DENVE

Food Crawls

Bre Patterson

TOURING *the* NEIGHBORHOODS
ONE BITE *&* LIBATION *at a* TIME

Globe
Pequot

GUILFORD, CONNECTICUT

Globe
Pequot

An imprint of The Rowman & Littlefield Publishing Group, Inc.
4501 Forbes Blvd., Ste. 200
Lanham, MD 20706
www.rowman.com

All photos by the author unless otherwise noted
Maps by The Rowman & Littlefield Publishing Group, Inc.

British Library Cataloguing in Publication Information available

Library of Congress Cataloging-in-Publication Data available

ISBN 978-1-4930-4512-9 (paper : alk. paper)
ISBN 978-1-4930-4513-6 (electronic)

♾™ The paper used in this publication meets the minimum requirements
of American National Standard for Information Sciences—Permanence of
Paper for Printed Library Materials, ANSI/NISO Z39.48-1992

Contents

Introduction

WELCOME TO DENVER—THE MILE HIGH CITY, the 303, and the 5,280—where we're guaranteed 300 days of sunshine every year and Denver Broncos–colored sunsets. At 5,280 feet above sea level, we're a mile closer to the sun and love soaking in the rays from the patios and rooftops. Denverites love the mountain views, with over 200 visible peaks.

We're true to our Wild West roots and remain the outlaws in the culinary scene. We close down major roads to throw food festivals like Top Taco or to dine alfresco in the summer on Larimer Street. We keep it real with our ingredients, support local farmers, and seek out the best-quality meats. Colorado lamb is on every menu and we grow our own vegetables in urban gardens.

We're a city with our own style; beanies and flannels are always acceptable even on a hot summer day. You will be hard-pressed to find a white-tablecloth restaurant here, because we love to keep it casual. The majority of restaurants in Denver are chef owned and driven, and those culinary masters rise to the challenge of creating interesting concepts and unique dishes.

We love the 303 so much that we have an annual celebration, 303 Day, to honor Denver every 3rd of March. We challenge you to not fall in love with Denver and its food scene after reading this book.

Follow the Icons

 If you eat something outrageous and don't take a photo for Instagram, did you really eat it? These restaurants feature dishes that are Instagram famous. These items must be seen (and snapped) to be believed, and luckily they taste as good as they look!

 Cheers to a fabulous night out in Denver! These spots add a little glam to your grub and are perfect for marking a special occasion.

 Follow this icon when you're crawling for cocktails. This symbol points out the establishments that are best known for their great drinks. The food never fails here, but make sure to come thirsty, too!

 This icon means that sweet treats are ahead. Bring your sweet tooth to these spots for dessert first (or second, or third).

 Denver is for brunch. Look for this icon when crawling with a crew that needs sweet and savory (or an excuse to drink before noon).

 Denver loves its meatless Mondays and meat reduced options. Look for this icon when crawling with vegans and vegetarians in your crew.

THE WEST HIGHLAND CRAWL

1. **EL CAMINO COMMUNITY TAVERN, 3628** W. 32nd Ave., Denver, (720) 889-7946, elcaminotavern.com

2. **SWEET COW ICE CREAM, 3475** W. 32nd Ave., Denver, (303) 477-3269, sweetcowicecream.com/denver-highlands

3. **HIMCHULI—INDIAN AND NEPALI CUISINE, 3489** W. 32nd Ave., Denver, (303) 728-9957, himchulidenver.com

4. **BLUE PAN PIZZA, 3930** W. 32nd Ave., Denver, (720) 456-7666, bluepandenver.com

5. **LEROY'S BAGELS, 4432** W. 29th Ave., Denver, (303) 477-0266, leroysbagels.com

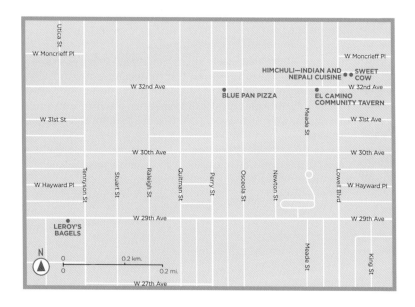

West Highland

The West Side Is the Best Side

ACROSS THE HIGHWAY FROM DOWNTOWN DENVER you will find The Highlands, home of the North High School Vikings, charming homes, and streets filled with overarching trees. When I first moved to Denver, I picked the West 32nd Avenue area to live because of its sense of community and the proximity to downtown. The homes range from quaint, original bungalows to renovated contemporary architecture. Newer homes capitalize on rooftop patios for the best views of the city skyline, while the older homes relish oversize yards. The Highlands Square is the gathering center for the neighborhood. Lined with boutiques, salons, fitness studios, bookstores, restaurants, and more, this area throws the best street festivals and hosts an artisanal farmers' market. It's a vibrant, hip, and family-friendly community. The locals can be found sipping a latte at Highland Cork and Café in the morning and margaritas at El Camino Tavern in the evening, strollers are packed with cheese boards from St. Kilian's Cheese & Market or a bottle of wine from Mondo Vino, and a walk down the street is not complete without a visit to The Perfect Petal.

1

EL CAMINO COMMUNITY TAVERN

A true local tavern, this tequila-forward watering hole is home to the neighbors of West Highland. **EL CAMINO'S** core foundation includes giving back to the schools, offering their employees opportunities to work toward their passions outside of work, and nourishing customers with sustainable, fresh ingredients. Everyone is family at El Camino, and if you don't know anyone, you will likely leave adopted by another customer. When entering, take note of the sign hanging above your head for directions on seating. Occasionally a "Seat Yourself" option is available and the best spot to snag is at the booths behind the bar, but more frequently a "Wait to Be Seated" sign indicates a waitlist.

El Camino is well known for their hot pink paisley napkins and street tacos, but the mac 'n' queso cannot be missed. It's a heaping bowl of large pasta shells and fried pickled jalapeños smothered in their famous house queso, topped with Cotija cheese, crema, pico de gallo, crushed tortilla strips, and cilantro. The toppings options seem to never end with the choice to add on carnitas, chicken, chorizo, portobello mushrooms, or shrimp.

Other menu favorites include mahi mahi ceviche, carnitas banh mi topped with jicama slaw, and churritos served with chocolate sauce

and tequila dulce de leche. The best way to eat through the menu is to order during happy hour, which is every day 3 p.m. to 6:30 p.m., with a late-night happy hour from 10 p.m. to close. Easily cross off the green chili nachos, shishito peppers, mini guac and queso, and jalapeño bottle caps from your list.

Their killer happy hour also includes El Camino's tequila-infused margaritas, wine by the glass, tequila shots, and beers. More daring customers can order the "Staff Pick" that has never done me wrong or the Deer-&-Beer, an imperial beer accompanied by a shot of Cazadores Blanco. Keeping to the tavern feel, El Camino serves cans of Tecate, PBR, and Coors Original as well as 10 rotating draft beers.

Weekly specials include $1 Taco Tuesday, 50 percent off bottles of wine on Wednesday, and weekend brunch on Saturday and Sunday from 10 a.m. to 2 p.m. with $2 mimosas and $3 Bloody Marys. Order the

TIP

If you visit frequently, you probably keep a seat warm at the bar. You may even have a stack of wooden nickels, a token of appreciation randomly given out by the staff, redeemable for a free drink.As the neighborhood expands, it is harder to come across these and can make a loyal customer stand out.

shrimp 'n' grits for a savory entree, or for a sweet tooth order the Dios Mio—brioche french toast topped with seared plantains, salted tequila dulce de leche, scrambled eggs, and bacon.

During West 32nd street festivals, El Camino parks a 1970s Chevrolet El Camino out front of the restaurant and grills food from the trunk. Yes, you read that correctly, there is a grill permanently in the trunk of the car serving street tacos and *elotes* (Mexican street corn). If the savory smells don't catch your attention, the flames and smoked meats will.

2

SWEET COW ICE CREAM

Cue the music, spin the disco ball, flip on the multicolored lights, and let the kids bounce on the spotted cows. **SWEET COW** throws the best party for customers waiting to order their scoops. They have become a neighborhood favorite for all ages. Adult delights like chocolate oatmeal stout and whiskey corn flake will satisfy a boozy sweet tooth, while kids and traditionalists will love classics like cookies and cream, Dutch chocolate, and pistachio. Sweet Cow offers 24 flavors daily with 9 staples available year-round. All of the ice cream can be served in a traditional sugar or waffle cone, or opt for the pretzel cone to complement the sweetness with something salty. One of my favorite orders is the pretzel cone with cookies and cream ice cream.

Sweet Cow's ice cream is made in house in small batches. This keeps the flavor creations limited in quantity and rotating with new options. Aside from ice cream cones, you can indulge in a locally brewed root beer float, milkshake, or a Moo-Good Sundae: two scoops topped with a choice of nuts, sprinkles, candy, hot fudge, caramel, and whipped cream.

If you don't have the time to stand in line, select from the to-go freezer. There are pints and quarts of ice cream, Ice Cream Sammies, and ice cream cakes. The best to-go option is the Ice Cream Sammie, two cookies holding a scoop of ice cream in between them. The cookies are made in house, like the ice cream. Chocolate chip cookies with cookies and cream ice cream are always available, but other varieties include snickerdoodle cookies with vanilla or chocolate chip cookies with Dutch chocolate. Get an ice cream cake to share Sweet Cow with friends. They have different sizes to feed 8, 12, or 24 with flavor options including cookie dough and cookies and cream.

Sweet Cow has been scooping smiles since 2013 on West 32nd. They offer four sorbet options and one or two vegan options. Weeknights they are open until 10 p.m. and weekends until 11 p.m. They have six locations and an ice cream truck for special events.

3 HIMCHULI—INDIAN AND NEPALI CUISINE

The Himalayas don't seem thousands of miles away with **HIMCHULI**'s authentic Nepali and Indian dishes found right in the center of West Highland. The smell of the authentic spices will draw you right through their door. The mouthwatering dishes are full of flavor that will keep you coming back to explore more menu options. My favorite tandoori bread is the lightly sweet Kabuli naan made with dates and nuts. I recommend starting with an appetizer like the chat samosa, a savory stuffed pastry with chickpeas, onion, tomato, yogurt, and tamarind chutney or the chicken momos, a steamed or fried dumpling. Then move onto the entrees. The masala is my favorite with the korma coming in close second. Opt for the sweet potato

masala to stay on the lighter side or the shrimp masala for a heartier meal. Be cautious about going above a 3 when asked what level you'd like your spice on a scale of 1 to 7. If you enjoy long-lasting heat, then a level 5 would be suitable.

New to Indian and Nepali food? Go to Himchuli for the daily lunch buffet. The third Tuesday of every month Himchuli offers a vegan buffet dinner with about six to eight courses. The buffet includes staples like the chana masala and saag tofu paneer. It's an opportunity for carnivores, meat reducers, vegetarians, and vegans to explore non-meat options from appetizers to dessert.

KG (Khagendra Jung Gurung) and his family own Himchuli as well as Indian and Nepali restaurants all over the Colorado Front Range. Originally from the Kathmandu valley of Nepal, KG takes pride in sharing his family's recipes for all to enjoy. He really has brought the Himalayas to the foothills.

4

BLUE PAN PIZZA

If you've never tasted Detroit-style pizza, this is a *must* stop. **BLUE PAN PIZZA** is the hottest place to be on a Monday night for the buy one, get one pizza. The average 2-hour wait is worth every second once you take your first bite into a slice of the award-winning Brooklyn Bridge Detroit-style pizza. Awarded first place in the Traditional Division at the International Pizza Challenge 2014, this specialty pan pizza is all the rage. The salty pepperoni and sausage complement creamy dollops of ricotta and a melted cheese blend—what pizza dreams are made of.

If you are going to order more than one type of specialty pizza, I highly recommend the Parma Italia, another first place award winner. This pan pizza has a combination of flavors from the prosciutto di Parma and sopressata to the burrata and smoked Scamorza cheeses.

All of the Detroit pizza dough is made with Pendleton high-gluten flour and cooked in a gas deck oven at 550 degrees. The flour, oven type, and temperature are taken very seriously for the perfect pizza at Blue Pan. It's even noted on the menu.

Detroit style isn't the only pizza they are tossing here. They pay homage to their neighbor across the lake with the "Chicago Cracker Thin" style. As a Chicago native, I greatly appreciate a good thin crust pizza that flakes away like a saltine cracker when you crunch into it. The Chicago style is cooked in an electric oven at 650 degrees and made with Cerasita flour from Chicago. Blue Pan offers only two options of the cracker thin—Louie Louie with Italian sausage, spinach, roasted garlic cloves, giardiniera peppers, cherry tomatoes, and chili oil—or the sausage and pepper with mixed bell peppers. fresh garlic, onions, Italian sausage, and giardiniera. The other crust options are New York slice, classic Italian, and gluten free.

I also highly suggest ordering the arugula salad with artichokes, shaved parmesan, and tomatoes, which includes a light oil and vinegar dressing and a dash of salt and pepper. My other must-try is harder to get your fork on. The homemade tiramisu is always on the menu, but rarely available. This mysterious and highly sought after dessert is a secret family recipe and made about once a month. I can promise you that even the smallest sliver of the tiramisu is worth asking for each time you visit.

5

LEROY'S BAGELS

Wait until you sink your teeth into one of the soft, chewy bagels at Leroy's. They delicately toast the bagels for crisp, not too crunchy edges and a soft inside. The bagels and cream cheeses are made fresh daily. They offer traditional bagels like everything, poppyseed, and plain as well as unique types like spinach and parmesan, jalapeño cheddar, and sun-dried tomato. Leroy's even has a plain and daily special flavored vegan, gluten-free bagel. I have tried the vegan options several times and think they are just as delicious as the glutenous bagels. The everything bagel is very

popular because it is so flavorful with its toasted black and white sesame seeds, poppyseeds, garlic, onion, and coarse sea salt. It pairs perfectly with the cucumber dill or honey cream cheese.

If you want to amp up your breakfast, there is a selection of bagel sandwiches to choose from or a build your own. My favorite is the lox sandwich with smoked salmon, plain cream cheese, capers, red onion, and tomato on an Asiago bagel. If I am craving eggs, I order the egg, meat, and cheese sandwich and swap out the cheese for the bacon, cheddar and chive cream cheese.

GET THERE EARLY!

Vegan and gluten-free bagels fly off the shelf by 10 a.m. If you really want to get your hands on one, you can order it in advance. While Leroy's is open until 2 p.m. for the lunch crowd, they can close early if they sell out.

THE BERKELEY CRAWL

1. **VITAL ROOT**, 3915 Tennyson St., Denver, (303) 474-4131, vitalrootdenver.com

2. **HOPS & PIE**, 3920 Tennyson St., Denver, (303) 477-7000, hopsandpie.com

3. **HIGH POINT CREAMERY**, 3977 Tennyson St., Denver, (720) 638-8697, highpointcreamery.com

4. **PARISI**, 4401 Tennyson St., Denver, (303) 561-0234, parisidenver.com/parisi

5. **TOCABE, AN AMERICAN INDIAN EATERY**, 3536 W. 44th Ave., Denver, (720) 524-8282, tocabe.com

6. **SCRATCH BURRITO & HAPPY TAP**, 4262 N. Lowell Blvd., Denver, (303) 477-3000, scratchburrito.com

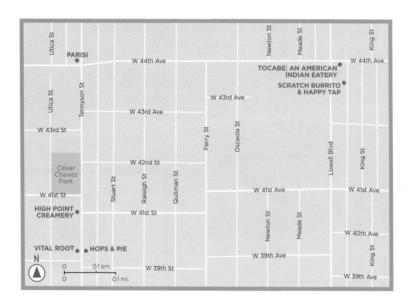

Berkeley

Totally Tennyson, for the Vibrant and Unique

THE BERKELEY NEIGHBORHOOD is best known for Tennyson Street, where you can eat the whole way down the street. It's lined with restaurants, pubs, bars, lounges, and even a music venue. This quiet neighborhood is only a few blocks long, but filled with character. Some of the historic buildings date back to the 1920s.

On any given day, the typical Berkeley neighbor can be found brunching at Vital Root, strolling through trendy boutiques like Inspyre, walking their pups to Mouthfuls, licking ice cream from High Point Creamery, catching happy hour at Scratch Burrito & Happy Tap, and enjoying a show at The Oriental Theater. Berkeley is a gem with a lot of spunk. The top event of the year is Totally Tennyson, a '70s and '80s–themed block party to raise money for the public school. It's a perfect theme for a neighborhood that retains the best of its past yet still has a modern vibe.

1

VITAL ROOT

Calling all health-conscious gastronomes! **VITAL ROOT** is the superhero of the Denver vegetarian food scene. Their tagline is "Fast (Slo) Food," meaning fresh, organic, healthy, free of pesticides and chemicals served in a fast casual setting, but not meant to make customers hurry through their tasting experience. Vital Root offers nourishing ingredients and affordable options while leading the way down the exploratory path of evolving food preferences. The dishes are inventive, vibrant in color, and playful on the palate.

The ambience at Vital Root is welcoming, airy, and modern. You can sunbathe on the front patio or take in the warmth from the shaded back patio. Owner/chef Justin Cucci works to use repurposed and recycled elements throughout the restaurant. The outdoor patio is lined with a ½-mile-long herb garden winding in front of the upcycled cafeteria trays that serve as a fence, and the glassware is made of recycled bottles. Vital Root is committed to sustainability. The restaurant is 100 percent wind-powered, they support over 55 local farmers, and grow more than 40 percent of the produce used in the restaurant in their own garden.

If you're visiting for brunch, I suggest ordering the coconut quinoa pancakes: sesame coconut crunch, hibiscus, blueberry-lemon compote, and maple syrup for just $9. Pair it with the beet bop cold-pressed juice or, for the more boozy palate, opt for the blood orange mimosa. Another favorite

available all day is the everything bagel avocado toast served on sunflower seed bread with a poached egg, goat cheese, smoked almonds, and a chili crunch. Customers rave about the everything seasoning, and you can take home the everything chickpeas from the grab and go section. My favorite lunch and dinner items are the banh mi tacos: edamame pâté, lemongrass tofu, pickled vegetables, cucumber, fresh herbs, jalapeño and sriracha aioli; or the Korean stir fry: yam noodles, brown rice, bok choy, red pepper, shiitake mushrooms, cashew and tamari-ginger sauce. Regardless of what I order I always order the beet brownie and the Korean barbecue veggie wings made with smoked broccoli and cauliflower, served with goddess ranch dip.

Let it be known that this is one of my favorite happy hour spots. Daily from 3 to 6 p.m. they serve $2 banh mi or avocado tacos, $3 Korean barbecue veggie wings, $4 cashew queso dip, and $4 house wine and cocktails. Most importantly the Vital Margarita will rock your salt rim off.

TIP

RAW POP-UP DINNER SERIES

Reserve your spot for Vital Root's four-course dinner the first Monday of every month. What's on the menu? It's a surprise until it is presented to you to eat. What's the price? A very reasonable $25. Prepare your senses to be tantalized.

2 HOPS & PIE

Just as the name says, this is the spot to stop for craft beer and artisan pizza. **HOPS & PIE** is a neighborhood favorite because it's family friendly, has a great vibe, the price is right, and it is run by two passionate owners, Drew and Leah Watson. The menu doesn't just have pizza but includes appetizers, salads, and sandwiches.

Hops & Pie breaks the barriers with their unfathomable combination of flavors that burst in your mouth. Take the slice of the day—burrito style: braised pork, beans and rice, pickled jalapenos and topped with avocado cream and pico de gallo. Another wild combo is black mission fig puree, applewood smoked bacon, and blue cheese finished with baby arugula and honey. Honey on pizza is a Colorado invention—it can't be described or explained. It's just something you have to experience. Don't go drizzling honey on any pizza—it's only suitable on certain styles of crust.

A beer keeper (styled after the iconic '90s Trapper Keeper) at every table lists the 22 rotating specialty beers from sour beers to malts. They also serve wine, for the rare diner unconvinced by this ever-tempting list.

Hops & Pie goes beyond pizza with some of the best sandwiches in town. They even were recognized in the local publication *Westword* for Best Sandwich at a Non-Sandwich Shop. My go-to is the pulled pork sandwich. The hickory-smoked pulled pork is glazed in Thai chili and pineapple with

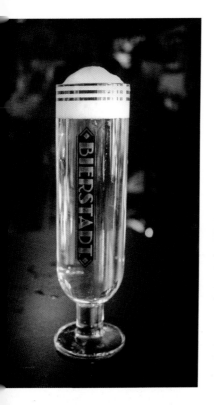

a spicy slaw on top. There's also the heartier IPA mac 'n' cheese: a heaping portion of macaroni mixed with the house IPA, cheddar, and smoked ham, then topped with English peas and herbed bread crumbs.

A visit to Hops & Pie isn't complete without dessert. It's a toss-up between the bread pudding and the Super Treat. If gooey bourbon sauce and vanilla ice cream on top of warm dough is calling your sweet tooth, don't pass the bread pudding up. Otherwise if you're seeking a taste of childhood with a twist, then the Super Treat will send you down memory lane. It's a mixture of peanut butter Cap'n Crunch and Cocoa Puffs held together with marshmallows for a sticky and sweet crispy treat.

WHAT'S THE SECRET TO THE GREAT-TASTING PIZZA?

It's all in the (beer) dough! A perfect 50/50 mixture of water and the house IPA makes the dough chewy with little air bubbles. The crust comes in traditional, pan, and Detroit style. Don't forget to pair it with a draft beer.

3

HIGH POINT CREAMERY

At most Denver street festivals, there's a hot pink ice cream truck named Big Pinky and a little ice cream chest on wheels named Lil' Woodie. Big Pinky and Lil' Woodie come from **HIGH POINT CREAMERY**, which has a few locations throughout downtown. The ice cream is adventurous with flavors like Tincup whiskey and pistachio brittle, Earl Grey and shortbread, or basil with blackberry swirl. The best way to sample all the flavors is to split a flight with a friend. It's your choice of five ice cream flavors and choice of hot fudge or caramel, served with a little triangle of waffle cone.

High Point was dreamt up by husband and wife duo Erika Thomas and Chad Stutz. Her culinary and his business backgrounds melded together to create one of Denver's beloved ice cream shops. Their mission is to use happy ingredients, to make happy ice cream, while developing happy employees, in order to make you a happy customer.

TASTE INVENTORS NEEDED!

If you think you can come up with an eclectic pairing, then submit the combination to High Point through Instagram. They often hold contests to guess the next flavor based on ingredient pictures. This is an opportunity to hear all the funky flavors people submit for future inspiration.

4 PARISI

You don't have to take an international flight to enjoy the tastes of Florence, Italy, when **PARISI** has a plethora of authentic Italian food. Owners Simone and Christine Parisi moved to Denver in the late '90s and shared their Italian culture through the Parisi Italian Market & Deli. Within a year they outgrew the space and turned their focus toward a sit-down eatery instead of a marketplace. They made a slight name change to just Parisi and moved in to their current Tennyson Street space. Parisi is warm and inviting, mostly from the large wood-fired pizza on display for all to see. The space is open and filled with natural light and wraps around the corner with large windows.

When you enter this neighborhood staple, prepare for an experience that is all about food. Each menu item has a story behind it from the owners' life in Italy.

If you love paninis then you have to get one here, but they only serve them during lunch. The panini menu is endless and some are served as a traditional hot griddle-pressed sandwich while others are on thick focaccia bread. Paninis are owner Simone's favorite hometown food, so you can trust me when I say he makes a mean panini. The Piadina Romagnola Panini is prosciutto, arugula, and Stracchino (an Italian cheese) on a wood-fired flatbread; the Porchetta Panini has thin-sliced herbed and wood-fire-roasted pork loin with arugula, tomato and spicy aioli on a brioche bun.

Down the faintly illuminated stairs from the Parisi parking lot entrance is Firenze a Tavola, "Florence at your table," an intimate multicourse fine dining restaurant. The menu changes seasonally, but you can always find classic Italian dishes. It is open Wednesday through Saturday and reservations are strongly encouraged online.

The real reason I have to visit Parisi is to cure my craving for the pizza salad. It's a wood-fired pizza dough with melted mozzarella (and the option to add chicken) topped with chilled mixed greens, tomatoes, red onions, capers, oregano, feta, cucumbers, and olives that are tossed in a Caesar dressing. The pizza crust is folded in half like a sandwich and cut into triangles. The crust on top and bottom makes it like a pizza salad sandwich. It's the best combination for just $12. If you just want a good Italian wood-fired pizza, then they have the staples like Margherita, la diavola, and 3 formaggi.

You will swoon over Parisi once you try their homemade desserts like the pistachio or stracciatella gelato, the traditional or chocolate cannolis, and my favorite the tiramisu. If you fall in love with the authentic Italian food, you can even take it home with you from the small marketplace of imported Italian goods. They carry a small sampling of everything from pastas and dressings to chocolates and coffee.

5

TOCABE, AN AMERICAN INDIAN EATERY

American Indian cuisine may seem unfamiliar at first, but it's everyday foods presented in different combinations—think squashes, beans, rice, and meats. It's more approachable than expected. The spices, flavors, and combinations of ingredients make this cuisine delectable. **TOCABE**, An American Indian Eatery is a tasting experience through history and an exploration through flavors.

Notice the three hands on the wall that represent the three villages of the Osage nation: Pawhuska, Grayhorse, and Hominy. Tune your ears to the Indigenous music jamming over the speakers. It isn't the typical flute and drumming; it's music from Indigenous artists covering all genres like rap, blues, country, and even heavy metal. The staff members represent different tribal nations. If it isn't the ambience or the food that keep customers coming back, it's the staff and their excitement to share their culture.

The menu is made of staff favorites on one side and broken down by the type of dish on the other. The customer favorite is Bison Ribs: cured then braised in house-made bison stock, glazed and grilled with berry barbecue sauce, and served with two frybread biscuits. Grilling the ribs builds the flavor complexity and caramelizes the outside with the perfect char.

It creates a crispy top layer with juicy, tender bison underneath. The ribs don't need the berry barbecue sauce drizzle if dry rub style is preferred. However, it adds the perfect touch of tangy sweetness to the heat of the meat.

Frybread, the most popular item, is included in almost all of the dishes. It is a puffy dough made of beautiful air pockets, stretchy when pulled apart and chewy when bitten into. It is made fresh throughout the day in small batches. My favorite dish is the Indian Taco. The base layer is a piece of warm frybread and layered with black beans, hand-shredded bison,

lettuce, Osage hominy salsa, and sweet corn salsa. The employees will walk anyone through the menu, but for less adventurous diners there are more familiar options like the grilled chicken and ground beef.

Since opening, cofounders Ben Jacobs and Matt Chandra have traveled throughout the Indian country and brought recipes from other tribal nations into their restaurant. These recipes have been fine-tuned and incorporated with the original Osage recipes that were handed down from Ben's grand-mother. This is their way of trying to keep the food culture of more than 500 American Indian tribes alive.

In the United States American Indian cuisine is the oldest cui-sine and the only cuisine without a European influence. It has long waited to be the next trending cultural cuisine. Until that craze comes, Tocabe continues to be a kitchen by community, where all can gather and submit their rec-ipes to be shared. They prioritize Native-produced items first and local items second.

The history of frybread is complicated. It is a reminder of the hardships for the American Indians during early colonizations, when they had hunting and gathering restrictions and were given food rations. Frybread is an important symbol of perseverance for the Native American culture and is seen as a way to introduce American Indian cuisine in the pres-ent. It brings communities together at powwows, friends and family gather-ings, or at Tocabe, where it educated a city of people.

6 SCRATCH BURRITO & HAPPY TAP

Welcome to Berkeley neighborhood's stomping ground, **SCRATCH BURRITO & HAPPY TAP**. This fast-casual restaurant feels like a neighborhood block party every day—where customers play yard games in the parking lot, sit with new friends at the community picnic tables, or throw back a drink on the Adirondack chairs. This is where the "Happy Tap" name comes from. It's not just the outdoor fun that brings the locals in; it's the unique flavors and spin on a typical burrito with scratch ingredients. Chef/owner Clay Markwell is passionate about the Berkeley neighborhood and wanted to create a place that brought good food and the community together.

His menu is driven to create a single harmonious bite, to taste all the ingredients. The vehicle for that are the pound and a half burritos. Yes, they're heavy; everything is mixed instead of layered. Menu items #1 through #4 are traditional flavors for those playing it safe, and #5 through #8 are for the adventurous. The #5 Tandoori Lamb includes curried brown rice, dill pickle salad, cilantro raita, and crispy onions, and the #8 Blackened

Catfish has pico de gallo, red beans and rice, with Old Bay slaw. The menu captures all of the cuisines that are near and dear to Markwell's heart. All burritos can be made vegetarian, or swapped for a bowl or salad for a gluten-free or vegan option.

Scratch is more than burritos though. The menu includes appetizers, salads, quesadillas, and soups. The Ahi Poke Tostadas with yellowfin tuna, avocado, seaweed, and smoked ancho aioli can be eaten as a meal or an appetizer. The flavors are refreshing with a hint of spice from the aioli. The Vietnamese Chicken Wings are covered in a sweet and tangy sauce with chili, ginger, lime, garlic, and fish sauce. They pair great with a beer.

My favorite thing about Scratch is the cocktails. Like the weekly specials, the cocktails are driven by the herbs and ingredients that are bought off of the farmers' truck every Saturday. Blackberry mojitos, blood orange Old Fashioneds, and rosemary margaritas are a sampling of what you can expect.

TIP

KICK TO THE TASTE BUDS

The #7 is a must-order for first timers: Korean barbecue beef, fried rice, kalbi sauce, kimchi, and fried egg. The fried rice is made with fresh jalapeños, cabbage, carrots, and onions. Need to kick it up a notch on the heat? Add the WTF Hot Sauce on top. It has the six hottest peppers, grown by a local farmer specifically for Scratch.

THE SUNNYSIDE CRAWL

1. **THE UNIVERSAL**, 2911 W. 38th Ave., Denver, (303) 955-0815, theuniversaldenver.com

2. **BUCHI CAFE CUBANO**, 2651 W. 38th Ave., Denver, (303) 458-1328, buchicafecubano.com

3. **ILLEGAL PETE'S**, 1851 W. 38th Ave., Denver, (720) 400-7744, illegalpetes.com

4. **HUCKLEBERRY ROASTERS**, 4301 N. Pecos St., Denver, (866) 558-2201, huckleberryroasters.com

5. **BACON SOCIAL HOUSE**, 2434 W. 44th Ave., Denver, (720) 550-7065, baconsocialhouse.com

Sunnyside

It's Always Sunny for Breakfast

GOOD MORNING FROM SUNNYSIDE, where old meets new in the interiors and very few exteriors have been renovated. You will rarely find a tourist in this part of town because they flock to the hot, trendy restaurants. Secretly, Sunnyside is home to some culinary gems and a great breakfast scene. Locals peruse boutiques such as Denver Fashion Truck and Intrigue while waiting to get in to brunch at Bacon Social House. 38th and 44th Avenues are the most popular streets, while the streets in between are filled with ranch-style homes. Sunnyside is a true locals neighborhood. They bring the community together every year through the Sunnyside Music Festival, which raises money for aspiring young musicians.

1

THE UNIVERSAL

One might miss this trendy breakfast joint because it blends into the rest of a gray brick strip mall. **THE UNIVERSAL** is also the one tenant without a neon sign announcing their business. However, the two-pane window-cling has the logo splashed across it with brunch and lunch to cue their offerings. There's also a large brick patio wall that shades diners from the busy Federal Avenue.

TIP

Order the custard toast as soon as you sit down. It is bread soaked in nutmeg custard overnight, griddled and baked, then garnished with seasonal fruit. It's massive and could be shared between a table of four as an appetizer. It takes 20 minutes to make from the time of ordering.

There is rarely a waitlist longer than 25 minutes unless it's the weekend after 10:30 a.m. The Universal politely has on every table a notice that while diners may want to take their time, there are others waiting and they request you are polite to those waiting in line since it was once them. While I have never witnessed them ejecting anyone, the notice is friendly enough and keeps the flow of the restaurant moving.

While waiting for your table, you can walk up to the pastry case to order a brunch cocktail or coffee while you wait. This not only helps the wait time fly by, but it also cures your thirst. You can also look over the specials on the chalkboard or decide what you will eat.

The staff knows my order, the two egg standard: two eggs over medium, substitute avocado for meat, and substitute a biscuit for toast. I have a serious obsession with the house-made biscuits: buttery, fluffy, and doughy on the inside with a crispy outside. It steams all the way from the kitchen to the table. I split it in half and spread the house-made jam on it. The jam flavors are seasonal and usually there are different flavors every few tables so I scope out which jam I'm going to enjoy while waiting to be seated. The sweet and tangy strawberry rhubarb is my favorite jam.

If it's your first visit, I highly recommend ordering the Universal: two eggs any style, choice of meat, potatoes or grits, and a plain pancake. However, I'd substitute a banana pancake for the plain pancake and add on the Korean-style hanger steak. The Universal is a great way to sample the whole menu and will leave you full. Lunch is served only on weekdays. The banh mi sandwich with marinated tempeh will make your mouth shift to devour power mode. It has pickled vegetables, sambal mayo, arugula, and cilantro on a griddled baguette. If I share my excitement and love for The Universal any further, I might need an intervention.

2 BUCHI CAFE CUBANO

Nestled between two dispensaries—don't forget this is Colorado—is a bright red brick building with two large windows with the gold name, **BUCHI CAFE CUBANO**, across them. You will be greeted with a large patio and then the front door. Step inside to the bar that serves coffee and cocktails. The walls are painted marigold yellow and Denver Bronco orange. The bar is covered in tin slats around the bottom and solid oak on the top. This is a no-frills, authentic Cuban restaurant serving delicious food. Come for the rich Cuban flavors; skip taking photos because the food is not made for Instagram, just your belly.

The menu is short and sweet, offering only a small array of sandwiches, breakfast sandwiches, sides, and Cuban-style coffee drinks. I think the cocktail menu might be as large as the food menu with mojitos, caipir-

inha, and local beers from The Post, their sister restaurant. On Sunday they offer all-day happy hour and authentic Cuban plates like empanadas and flan.

The most remarkable sandwich is the *Aye Conyo*: Cuban roasted pork, ham, turkey, and pepperoni with Swiss cheese, pickles, onions, hot peppers, mustard, and key lime mayo. It's the best $11 I've ever spent. Pair it with one of their tasty mojitos made with real sugarcane and you will leave feeling a little more Cuban than when you arrive. You will also need to order a cafe con leche: three parts steamed milk, one part Cuban espresso, and raw sugar mixed together. It's an experience to awaken your soul.

Other favorites are the chicken empanadas with chimichurri for just $6 and the guava and cream cheese turnover from the dessert menu.

If you are short on time, you can bring the Cuban feast with you by ordering ahead for takeout. Buchi Cafe Cubano is family friendly and has something on the menu for everyone including vegetarians.

3 ILLEGAL PETE'S

This is one of the top late-night stops on any route home. When the bars are closing and you need to satisfy your hunger, prepare to line up at Illegal Pete's. The atmosphere is lively and everyone makes friends while waiting in the food line and sharing their funniest memories from previous visits. **ILLEGAL PETE'S** is the neighborhood spot to come as you are. One time I showed up after a murder mystery party dressed as a fortune teller with a third eye painted on my forehead. It started a conversation followed by an in-line dance-off. If you want to eat like a local, then this is one spot you can't miss.

While the same great-tasting food is at every Illegal Pete's, they each have their own individuality when it comes to the staff, music, and neighborhood vibe. This is what their mission statement is all about: "We celebrate humanity. We celebrate individuality. We celebrate relationships and connections. And most importantly, we celebrate every human's need for tasty food, stiff drinks and good times. Well, maybe it's not a need, but it's certainly a want. Either way, it's our desire to make each Illegal Pete's location the kind of place where you can go to celebrate more with other humans."

The menu is Tex-Mex style offering classics like bowls, burritos, nachos, tacos, and salads. However, Pete's Specialties include all my favorites

TIP

Headed to a party or a business meeting? Show up with a case o' queso! Thirty ounces of liquid gold (aka queso) served with fresh chips. This thing is almost as unbelievable as Bigfoot!

and take a few extra minutes of love to build the perfect entree. The taquitos, crispy little rolls of deliciousness, come with chopped chicken or shredded beef, then topped with melted cheese and your choice of sour cream or guacamole. Pro-tip: order the six taquitos with three beef and three chicken to maximize the variety of flavors. Add a side of green chili and queso. Another specialty is the Baja-style fish tacos with beer-battered fish topped with cabbage, salsa fresca, lime, and zesty ranch dressing. Other specialties include the grilled quesadilla, smothered burrito, and potato filling instead of rice.

While Illegal Pete's is quick service for food, the bar is a place where you will want to hang out all day. All bar patrons get bottomless chips and salsa with the order of an alcoholic beverage. I always add on queso and guacamole in an attempt to have to be rolled out the door from being satiated. They also have a very generous daily happy hour from 3 to 8 p.m. with house margaritas, cocktails, local drafts, and a selection of bottled beers from Mexico. The selections are different at each Illegal Pete's because each location features their favorites. I mean, that isn't a crime!

4

HUCKLEBERRY ROASTERS

Whitewashed brick walls covered in murals by local artists give this coffee roastery a mid-modern style. The black metal and natural wood bookshelves house a variety of items to purchase, from T-shirts to bags of coffee beans.

HUCKLEBERRY ROASTERS started out in a garage as a side hustle and has grown into a multilocation coffee shop. The people behind Huck are passionate not only about the roastery but the community. Sunnyside is the original location and was well received by the neighborhood

when they moved in. Off the corner of 43rd and Pecos is their large corner-lot building with a garage door that opens across the front to let the smell of the roastery fume out. The picnic tables on the patio are for the community to sit and enjoy coffee together while the two-person tables on the inside attract remote workers and students.

From the staff to the head roasters, every employee is proud of the coffee. It can be heard in their description of the different roasted blends and it can be seen in the latte art. The case is always filled with pastries from different local bakeries. It is Huck's way of supporting the local bakers.

On a hot afternoon, I love a pick-me-up iced Americano with a dash of caramel syrup paired with a chocolate croissant. On a cold winter morning, I opt for a cup of coffee and a muffin. I love Huckleberry so much that I drink out of a mug I purchased from them once a week when it is not filled with a mini bouquet of flowers.

5

BACON SOCIAL HOUSE

"Peace, Love, Bacon, and More Bacon" is the motto at **BACON SOCIAL HOUSE**. This establishment's name comes from the option to add bacon to any entree or even cocktail, and bacon is always good anytime. Start with a Bacon Flight of six flavors: applewood, barbecue, candied, habañero, paleo, and the flavor of the day. Make your way into the Bacon Hash: hickory-smoked country bacon, poached egg, sweet potato, roasted Hatch chiles, caramelized onion, and tomato aioli.

BSH is a three-time winner of the Diner's Choice Award from Open-Table; it's no wonder why Denverites crave the food here. They're open for brunch and dinner 7 days a week. That means you don't have to wait until the weekend to make brunch plans. The menu is crafted to easily transition from day to night offerings. The Between the Buns evening menu can be found under the Sammies and Burgers brunch menu.

Brunch-centered items include chicken and waffles: Belgian waffle, signature sausage gravy, crispy fried chicken breast, with a side of applewood-smoked bacon; or the Whole Hog Omelet with pulled pork, applewood-smoked bacon, ham, cheddar, sourdough toast or Wolferman's English muffin, tomatillo salsa, served with the choice of tots or fries.

They don't let any guest go thirsty while waiting for a table. Complimentary coffee is served at the front door and there's a pop-up bar cart for cocktails in the waiting area. Cocktails come as a single glass or by the carafe. Order the St. Bacon: sparkling wine, St. Germain, fresh lemon juice, lavender, and bubbles. It's light, boozy and tantalizing on the taste buds.

All-day items include the savory Iron Skillet Jalapeño Cornbread served with warm butter; the BLT—Habañero & Waffle Style: cheddar waffle, thick-cut and habañero bacon, tomato, lettuce, and avocado mayo; or the lighter options such as the beet salad: mixed greens, beets, goat cheese, candied walnuts, strawberries, and shallot vinaigrette.

THE LOHI CRAWL

1. **JUST BE KITCHEN**, 2364 15th St., Denver, (303) 284-6652, justbekitchen.com

2. **MASTERPIECE DELICATESSEN**, 1575 Central St., Denver, (303) 561-3354, masterpiecedeli.com

3. **EL FIVE**, 2930 Umatilla St., Fifth Fl., Denver, (303) 524-9193, elfivedenver.com

4. **LITTLE MAN ICE CREAM**, 2620 16th St., Denver, (303) 455-3811, littlemanicecream.com

5. **POSTINO**, 2715 17th St., Denver, (303) 433-6363, postinowinecafe.com

6. **THE WELL PIZZA & BAR**, 3210 Wyandot St., Denver, (303) 999-3590, thewelldenver.com

LoHi

Lo Patios and Hi Rooftops

BUSTLING BARS, BOUTIQUES, AND SMALL BUSINESSES spread like wildfire over the past few years in LoHi, the Lower Highlands. As more people move in, the food scene is becoming more diverse. The food scene is the wildest in this neighborhood with dietary restriction–friendly restaurants like Just BE Kitchen and El Five. The patios and rooftops are slammed with people meeting friends, savoring a work happy hour at Postino, or experiencing their first Tinder date.

1

JUST BE KITCHEN

Nourish your soul with every mindful bite at **JUST BE KITCHEN**, a fast-casual kitchen serving gluten-, grain-, and sugar-free comfort food. When you are here, you are important to everyone, including the other diners. People share their stories about how JBK has changed their lives with their holistic recipes. The menu is fully transparent and most items can be modified for dietary restrictions or sensitivities. I have met new friends at JBK from casual conversations and seeing them there frequently. The best friendship I have made is with the founder/CEO/chief foodie officer Jennifer Peters. She quit her corporate job and put everything into this restaurant to enable others to reach their highest potential through mindful mouthfuls.

The menu is kind-hearted like Peters, with entrees named after positive states of being. The Fulfilled is a breakfast burrito made with scrambled eggs, sausage, vegan cheddar wiz, and sweet potato hash wrapped in a paleo almond tortilla and smothered in pork or veggie green chili. Fulfilled is the bestseller and available for lunch and dinner with a few swaps to the ingredients. The almond tortilla is craze worthy. Everyone wants the recipe and since it's a secret, everyone wants a fridge full of them. Good thing you can order it as a side.

The menu changes with the seasons and chef Chase Eliot is to thank for the inventive dishes. A

couple of entrees are always available like Fulfilled; Wonder, a seasonal veggie hash with almond gremolata, sweet potato whip, and poached egg; Crave, a 100% grass-fed burger with pulled pork, house pickles, baconaise, and arugula served on a house bun; and Divine, a brownie trifle with crème anglaise. Believe me when I say that if the Divine ever leaves the menu, JBK is going to need an army to hold back the crowd for the last bite. The brownie is gluten free and chocolaty. It's chopped into little squares with layers of the crème anglaise in between. It is a must try when you visit.

Just BE Kitchen is also a coffee shop. Their espresso machine can whip up any beverage or you can order one of the unique lattes such as the Adaptogenic Mushroom Latte: seven-blend adaptogenic mushroom, mocha syrup and vanilla; or the CBD Cinnamon Latte: drip coffee, cinnamon, vanilla, honey, and CBD oil. My favorite drink, not because of the name, is the BEyoncé: sparkling water mixed with maple, cayenne, and lemon. It will kick you into gear any time. There's also the Collagen Creamsicle made with coconut milk, orange juice, tonic water, orange essential oils, and ice.

If you happen to see two pups blocking the back patio door, that's Oreo and Savi, the BEauties of Just BE Kitchen and unofficial mascots. They show up to work with Peters every day for belly rubs and cuddles from patrons. Did I mention the patio is dog friendly?

TIP

Check the events happening at Just BE Kitchen on the website. There's everything from self-defense classes and group workouts to meditation and goal-setting classes.

2 MASTERPIECE DELICATESSEN

The sandwiches at **MASTERPIECE DELI** are a knock out of the park. Soft, chewy bread and fresh-cut meats make for a marvelous experience. Executive chef/owner Justin Brunson opened this small fast-casual joint in 2008 with a focus on locally sourced and house-made ingredients. His mission: to make fine dining between bread. He doesn't compromise on any ingredients, quality, or portions. The meats are house-roasted, -braised and -cured. The food is top-notch, as good as you would get at a fine dining establishment.

Step up to the counter to order your breakfast or lunch. The smoked turkey sandwich has been a bestseller for years. It's smoked turkey breast, brie cheese, seasonal pears, arugula, and cranberry honey served on toasted wheat bread. The sandwich stands tall and will need two hands to hold. Another best seller is the Reuben: braised corned beef, sauerkraut, swiss, and Thousand Island dressing on toasted rye. Each deli sandwich is served with a choice of side: pasta salad, coleslaw, fresh fruit salad, or Zapp's Potato Chips. For an Americana classic, the gourmet grilled cheese sandwich is served with a choice of two cheeses on bread. There's even the option to add sautéed wild mushrooms, fresh spinach, local free-range fried egg, bacon, fresh tomato or caramelized onions.

Chef Justin makes it hard to skip a visit to Masterpiece because there is always a killer special of the day. Previous daily sandwiches have included River Bear Beef Brisket: Pepper Jack cheese, caramelized onions, sautéed wild mushrooms, piquillo peppers and roasted garlic aioli on a baguette; and the River Bear Corned Beef: melted cheddar, fried egg, hollandaise, and arugula served on a toasted brioche.

Once your order is placed, find a spot inside at the window or enjoy the shaded patio with views looking over the highway and the LoDo neighborhood. The main pedestrian bridge from LoDo to LoHi is right in front of Masterpiece's patio and is one of the best people-watching spots in town.

TIP

This is a small shop, so find your spot early to enjoy a long happy hour. Daily from 3 p.m. to 7 p.m. the menu includes deals on beers, wine, and cocktails.

The menu visible in the image includes:

TRADITIONAL TAPAS

PATATAS BRAVAS GF/V
CHORIZO, SALSA BRAVA,
GARLIC AIOLI, SHERRY GASTRIQUE

GOAT CHEESE CROQUETTAS
CRISPY JAMÓN, FRISÉE,
MARCONAS, MASTIC CHILI HONEY

SARDINE BRUSCHETTA* GF
IBERICO MORCILLA, GARLIC CH
ORANGE, TOMATO SHERRY SAUCE
CIABATTA

SHRIMP & CALAMARI

CAMEROS CHEESE 4 WAYS GF   18
QUESO FLAN, ESPELETTE TUILE,
CRUMBLE, HONEYCOMB, APRICOTS,
MARCONAS, QUINCE JAM

SPREADS OF THE MED GF/V   20
PEANUT & CHARRED CARROT HUMMUS,
MUHAMMARA, TURKISH EGGPLANT,

3

EL FIVE

Unobstructed, panoramic views from the mountains to the city skyline make **EL FIVE** an iconic spot for visitors to see everything Denver has to offer. The menu focuses on Spanish and Mediterranean tapas with influences from the Middle East. It's a melting pot of the Mediterranean regions.

The dishes at El Five will take you on a tour of traditional, new school, and Middle Eastern tapas. Traditional items include goat cheese croquettes, patatas bravas, and spanakopita, while the new school has Turkish Pizza: pheasant confit, apricots, toum (garlic sauce), raisins, chestnuts, bitter greens, and chocolate jus; and dungeness crab: couscous, avocado, cucumber, sorrel, pistachio, and crème fraîche.

I only drink champagne on two occasions,
when I am in love and when I am not.

—Coco Chanel,
French fashion designer

El Five is my go-to place for celebrations, because who doesn't want to celebrate from the top of Denver—in fact, it's where I celebrated my engagement. The experience at El Five is meant to be shared with the ones you love. Start with Spread of The Med: peanut and charred carrot hummus, *muhammara* (red pepper spread),

Turkish eggplant, artichokes, and house-made pita are served alongside raw veggies and assorted nuts. This shareable platter is a taste through all the Mediterranean flavors you can expect during your visit.

Leave your resting brunch face at home! Every Sunday is a brunch party with bottomless tapas and mimosas. There's even a DJ to help you get into the boozy-brunch mood. Order the Apricot Froze or Blood Orange Mimosa. The tapas bar includes madeleines, tuna-stuffed Peppadews, miniature chocolate croissants, garlic shrimp with chiles, beignets, and more. The bottomless brunch also includes a choice of entree and a cocktail. I recommend the Sausage Paella: chorizo, lamb sausage, manchego, bomba rice, sunny-side up egg, aioli, and salsa verde or the Tres Leches French Toast: caramelized milk, red currants, sesame hibiscus crumble, and mint.

4 LITTLE MAN ICE CREAM

A massive, 28-foot-tall cream can sits on a hill in LoHi with a line of people down the block and sometimes around it. People are there to get their fix of homemade **LITTLE MAN ICE CREAM**. It's made in small batches and uses the finest, local ingredients. The vintage uniforms, big smiles, and ambience are meant to evoke nostalgia for a bygone era. Little Man Ice Cream is named after Peter "Little Man" Tamburello, the father of founder Paul Tamburello. Since Paul opened Little Man on July 4, 2008, it has become a neighborhood favorite and an iconic landmark for Denver.

Bistro lights are strung from one side of the patio to the other, setting a romantic mood. The tunes of Frank Sinatra, Ray Charles, B. B. King, and Billie Holiday serenade the customers. The community plaza that surrounds Little Man Ice Cream is made with cobblestones and hosts musical performances, movies, and more.

Step right up to the red-and-white-striped awning of the cream can for your samples of flavors such as Peanut Butter Fudge Oreo, Beegan Key Lime Pie, French Toast, Whopper, Blackberry Honey Goat Cheese, and S'mores. Little Man always has Salted Oreo available because that is their signature flavor. Order it as a scoop in a homemade waffle cone or as an ice cream sandwich.

If you're in a hurry, there is an express counter next to the kids' playground. It offers up to 8 unique flavors. They keep the sampling to a minimum to keep the flow of people going. Check the flavor board first because not all the flavors are the same as in the cream can.

> Denverites go crazy for Little Man Ice Cream.
> On a snowy day, there is a line.
> On a rainy day, there is a line.
> At midnight, there is a line.
> On a sunny day, there is a line around the block.

5

POSTINO

Wine and dine in a place that excels at both. **POSTINO** is a wine cafe and full-service restaurant melded into one. They offer high-quality wines at affordable prices and an array of food that pairs well.

Postino started its roots in Phoenix, Arizona, in a former 1940s post office, which gave it its name—*postman* in Italian. When they expanded the concept to Denver, they stuck with their vision of turning vacant, rundown buildings into truly special places. Postino fits right at home in the trendy, revamped LoHi building that was the former Denver Book Binding Company. The interior pays homage to its roots with the book wall; thousands of books are stacked floor to ceiling to create a funky wave look. The rest of the interior is fascinating, from the Star Wars–themed skateboards to the geometric-patterned pillows on the lounge chairs. The vibrant colored booths curve around the walls, while the spacious dining room houses mid-century modern chairs. Garage doors open the restaurant into a patio that can be enjoyed year-round with heaters for the winter and umbrellas for the summer.

Wine shelves display the vast selection of bottles throughout the restaurant. The wines by the glass list is extensive, but Postino makes all the wines approachable, even for a novice. Their wine list includes reds from Argentina, Spain, Italy, and Macedonia; and whites from New Zealand, South Africa, California, and Hungary. The wine menu is always rotating, so ask what the current staff favorite is.

Postino can't be discussed without bragging about the bruschetta boards. Each board has four customizable breads. Selections include brie, apple, and fig spread; warm artichoke spread; burrata, bacon, arugula, and tomato; piquillo pepper and goat cheese; and seasonal flavors. Need inspiration on which to pick? Eat with your eyes; bruschetta is found on every table. Postino is open for wine-filled happy hours with the $5 glasses of wine and pitchers of beer 'til 5 p.m. deal, brunch, and dinner.

Postino has two other downtown locations, on South Broadway and on Colorado Boulevard.

6

THE WELL PIZZA & BAR

This is my secret gem restaurant. The music is bumping, there's not an empty seat at the bar, customers are yelling at the sports on TV, and the smell of pizza invites your stomach to growl. **THE WELL PIZZA & BAR** was started by longtime friends owner/operator Dino Marchig and business partner Will Hunt.

Marchig grew up in his mother's pizzerias and fine-tuned his pizza skills in Naples, Italy. After his lease ended at his former establishment, Mile High Pizza, his grandmother offered her building in LoHi. A break on rent sounded nice, and since The Well Pizza & Bar opened its doors, it has been a hidden gem off the popular 32nd Avenue.

The Well started off as a pizza take-out and delivery spot, then added a bar with local beers and spirits. Specialty cocktails like the Paloma are made with San Pellegrino sodas and served in mason jars. Can't decide on a cocktail? Come for happy hour and drink your way through the libations with a side of garlic knots.

The pizza is what people come for, though. The dough is the most important part of having good pizza; consistency and keeping the recipe simple are Marchig's focus, but the secrets are cold water for the dough and adding a little bit of sugar to the sauce for sweetness. When you order, start with the garlic knots. They are perfect, crispy outside and chewy inside. You can experience the pizza dough in the knots and dip them in the marinara to taste the sweet sauce.

Continue making your way through the menu with a pound of hot wings. These wings are big, tender, and juicy. Dip them in the house-made ranch. Don't worry if someone sees you licking the last drop of ranch; everyone loves it.

Ordering a pizza is like picking a favorite kid. It's impossible so you choose both. I demand you order at least two pizzas because you will stuff yourself full and want more when you get home. Favorite pizzas are The Bronco: sausage, spinach, artichoke hearts and garlic; or The B.A.: meatball, garlic, and romano cheese. If you prefer to pick your own toppings, you can build your own or order the pizette, a personal-size pizza with up to three toppings.

THE WELL HAS A SECRET MENU.

Hopefully this doesn't give too much away.

Order the stuffed pizza: two layers of dough stuffed with fresh ingredients of your choice; or give your best shot at finishing the smothered calzone. The staff has yet to see someone finish this glorious meal. A simple look at the smothered calzone will make you hungry!

THE LODO CRAWL

1. **CITIZEN RAIL**, 1899 16th St. Mall, Denver, (303) 323-0017, citizenrail.com

2. **THE COOPER LOUNGE**, 1701 Wynkoop St., Denver, (720) 460-3738, cooperlounge.com

3. **MERCANTILE DINING & PROVISION**, 1701 Wynkoop St. #155, Denver, (720) 460-3733, mercantiledenver.com

4. **RHEIN HAUS DENVER**, 1415 Market St., Denver, (303) 800-2652, rheinhausdenver.com

5. **GUARD & GRACE**, 1801 California St. #150, Denver, (303) 293-8500, guardandgrace.com

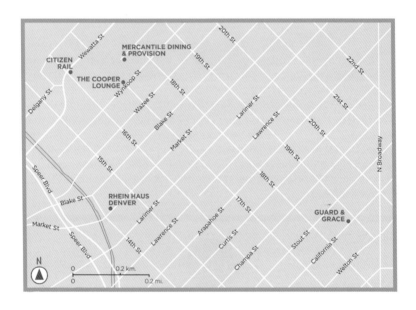

LoDo

The Low Down on the Food Scene

LODO, LOWER DOWNTOWN, IS THE HEART OF THE CITY and spans 23 blocks from Union Station to the top of the 16th Street Mall. Each street has its own identity, from the wall murals to the building architecture. The famous blocks are Union Station, Dairy Block, and Larimer Square. LoDo is packed with historic buildings: the Daniels and Fisher Tower, best known as the clock tower, the historic Morey Mercantile building that houses the Tattered Cover bookstore, and the Oxford Hotel that has been open since the 1890s.

Every street in LoDo is lively with pedestrians, bicyclists, and cars. It's the hub that connects all the neighborhoods through the light rail. The work crowd kicks off the morning hustle and the club crowd tucks the city in to sleep.

There are always lots of events happening in LoDo, from the various annual parades to the Christkindl market to the Denver Chalk Art Festival to dining alfresco on Larimer Street.

1 CITIZEN RAIL

A wood-fired grill and an open kitchen are the center of the dining room at **CITIZEN RAIL**. Though the restaurant is behind Union Station and attached to Hotel Born, it isn't only for hotel guests; locals visit frequently. Executive chef Christian Graves has been with the restaurant since it opened and is the tastemaker behind the seasonal menus. He sources local ingredients and is meticulous when it comes to sourcing meats. Next to the kitchen in a glass case is the dry-age room. Here there are meats on display like tomahawk steak and oxtails that will be on future menus. On the one-year anniversary of the restaurant Graves experimented with a 365-day dry-aged steak and placed it next to a 31-day dry-aged steak for the main entree. Sample the house-cured meats with the charcuterie board: truffled chicken liver mousse, fra'mani salami, American prosciutto, house pickle, and grainy mustard served with grilled bread.

Chef Christian has created some incredible dishes like my favorite appetizer From The Field: taro root chips, lemon hummus, beet relish, yogurt and herb dip, sunflower seeds, sprouts, and popped amaranth. He is always thinking of new ways to use the fire and different types of wood planks with the meat. He knocked it out of the park with the Mesquite-Fired Mussels,

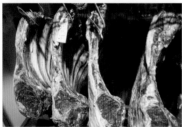

cooked over the fire and served in a creamy broth with dijon and tarragon. The grilled bread served on the side enhances the flavor because it absorbs the wood aromas from the grill.

Citizen Rail serves breakfast, weekend brunch, lunch, happy hour, and dinner. I love dining any time, because the menus share a few core items and present new items. For example, the lunch menu offers more sandwiches and bowls than the dinner menu. I've really enjoyed the Harissa Tofu Bowl: Israeli couscous, carrot, cauliflower, cashews, and sesame seeds for a lighter meal. The Citizen Rail Burger (applewood bacon, sharp cheddar, lettuce, tomato, and pickle served with malt fries) is an excellent choice for lunch, but is also available on the dinner menu.

The dessert is phenomenal and each dish includes homemade ice cream. The kitchen staff is always playing with new flavor combinations and trying to incorporate flavors that are in season. I can't name a favorite because it is always changing.

THE COOPER LOUNGE

A night on the town isn't complete without a stop at **THE COOPER LOUNGE**. This stylish lounge is on the second-floor mezzanine of Union Station, an intimate setting with the best views of people in transit below. The space is bright from the white walls and the extra-tall windows. Accent chairs and small couches make little nooks for groups of four or six to sit in their own space.

The cocktail menu is prestigious and the wine list is extensive. The Hibiscus Collins is made with Tanqueray gin, Hum liqueur, lemon, sugar, Q Drinks club soda, and beet brine. The flavor is surprisingly light with a hint of sweetness. Every drink is delivered on a silver platter with a side of complimentary nuts. If that is not enough to hold you over, club car cuisine is available at your table. The Antipasti Board is a selection of cured meats and artisanal cheeses served with paired accoutrements and artisan bread. The cart pulls up in front of you and you can point to the selection of cheeses or leave it to the chef. The showstopper is steak tartare. The prime sirloin is hand chopped then mixed with shallot and caper relish, tarragon béarnaise, and topped with quail yolk. The process is fascinating to watch.

Reservations are highly encouraged. Depending on the evening you might be able to walk up or add your name to the waitlist. You might be able to sit at the bar; however they keep those spots reserved on certain occasions.

3 MERCANTILE DINING & PROVISION

Chef Alex Seidel opened **MERCANTILE** as a place to explore culinary curiosities. When looking at spices, aren't you curious where they came from or how they were blended? What about coffee beans and the process behind them? Mercantile is the culmination of putting every step of the process together.

Seidel wanted to cure every meat, jar every preserve, and share the stories behind those ingredients. The open kitchen concept was thoughtfully planned so customers can start conversations about the processes behind the food they are making.

In the morning Mercantile is set as a market with a walk-up counter to place your order. I recommend the Ricotta Pancakes: seasonal jam, whipped ricotta, and pistachio granola; or the Avocado Quinoa Toast: cured salmon, sprouted lentil vinaigrette, and poached farmhouse egg. You can order these items to go or find a seat anywhere in the restaurant.

After five years in business executive chef Matt Vawter has taken the helm of Mercantile with an exceptional menu. The Short Rib is a rendition of the French onion soup that is begged for at his other concept restaurant, Fruition. The short rib is cooked in the soup broth. A favorite of mine is the Fried Chicken Bánh Mi: fried chicken, pickled vegetables, fish sauce vinaigrette, cilantro, mint, and jalapeño, on a baguette.

When the market quiets, the space turns into a fine dining restaurant in the evening with a completely different vibe. The dinner menu serves elevated comfort food with seasonally inspired dishes. The pastas are handmade. Swirl your fork into the Squid Ink Bucatini: squid, sofrito, and Ibérico bread crumbs, or order the family-style meals like the Smoked Lamb Shoulder, accompanied by grilled flatbread, chickpea hummus, and a seasonal vegetable. No matter what you order, you will eat one of the best dishes you'll ever have.

The wine program is a key focus at Mercantile. Sommelier Patrick Houghton has proven that wine doesn't need to be pretentious or expensive to enjoy. It should be an experience of different varietals and sharing the stories behind the winemakers.

4 RHEIN HAUS DENVER

Bocce ball, pretzels, and beers are just the start of what you can expect at **RHEIN HAUS**. This Bavarian-inspired restaurant serves food and fun all day and late into the night. The space is unique with two stories and six bocce ball courts. The interior decor has been sourced from around the world. The upstairs bar mantel is from a former bar in Germany and the chandeliers were sitting in a warehouse for years before they could find a place to call home.

The beer selection makes this the ultimate biergarten. There are more than 20 German, Belgian, and American beers available. Order a 12-ounce, half-liter, or liter of beer. Just like in Bavaria, beers come in large. If you can't decide which beers to try, order a flight with a sample of four beers.

The menu is everything you would expect out of a Bavarian restaurant: pretzels, mini brats, cheddarwurst sausage sliders, and wurst plates. Go big and order the Grillwurst Schmankerl plate with an almost 2-pound sampler of all the sausages offered with sauerkraut and mashed potatoes. I wouldn't try to eat it alone. However, the sausages are all made in house and too delicious to pass up.

For a true experience of Rhein Haus, order either the Smörgåsbord: a full *schweinshaxe* (ham hock), roasted bone-in chicken breast, Polish kiel-

basa, mashed potatoes, cheesy spaetzle, sauerkraut, and braised red cabbage; or the Pork Schnitzel: pork cutlet, pretzel breading, lemon caper parsley, shallot butter sauce, Granny Smith apple slaw, and charred lemon.

Once you've eaten your fair share of meat and drank enough beers, it's time to start thinking about dessert. The fresh-baked apple strudel is to drool for: flaky pastry filled with apples, golden raisins, graham cracker crumbs, and cinnamon that is dusted with confectioners' sugar. Or throw back some schnapps.

5

GUARD & GRACE

GUARD & GRACE is named after owner/chef Troy Guard's daughter. It's a modern steakhouse with an open kitchen, several private dining rooms, and a 4,000-bottle wine cellar. They provide top-notch service and take pride in each dish.

The front of the steakhouse opens to a lounge and bar, typically filled with people on the waitlist. Then it opens into the dining room filled with booths and tables. If you look toward the kitchen there is a chefs' bar. This is my preferred spot to sit because you can chat with the chefs and try small samples of what they're making. The raw bar is right there, so you may get lucky and try an oyster or jumbo shrimp on the house.

Start with the prime beef tartare: scallion yogurt, black truffle hollandaise fried egg, crispy parmesan, pickled shallot, and oak-fired carrots, with herb yogurt, fennel herb salad, and pistachio crumble. For an entree I suggest the Filet Mignon Flight: 4-ounce prime, 4-ounce angus, 4-ounce grass-fed. It's a unique way to try the same cut of meat from cows with different diets. There is a huge difference in taste. Seafood lovers must try the Alaskan Black Cod with charred broccolini, sweet soy butter, and sesame seeds.

After dinner, order a bottle of wine and enjoy dessert. The sweet corn crème brûlée is indescribable with popped sorghum, huckleberry ice cream, and caramel glass. A more indulgent dessert is the Triple Chocolate Bombe: malted milk chocolate, espresso caramel, and salted pretzel ice cream.

THE RINO CRAWL

1. **LOS CHINGONES**, 2463 Larimer St., Denver, (303) 295-0686, loschingonesmexican.com

2. **SUPER MEGA BIEN**, 1260 25th St., Denver, (720) 269-4695, supermegabien.com

3. **STOWAWAY KITCHEN**, 2528 Walnut St. #104, Denver, (720) 583-5481, stowawaydenver.com

4. **CALL**, 2845 Larimer St., Denver, (303) 954-0230

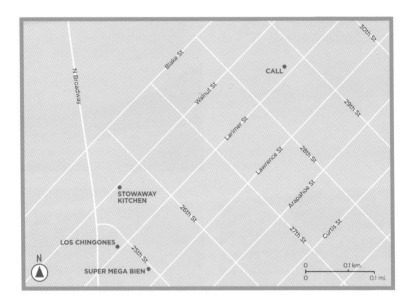

RiNo

Taste beyond the Boundaries

STREET ART DEFINES RINO (RIVER NORTH). It once was a neighborhood no one talked about because the streets were lined with empty warehouses. However in the past few years, the warehouses have been renovated to make room for breweries, art studios, food halls, fitness studios, and more. The graffiti was replaced with wall murals and the neighborhood has become livelier. Every September artists from around the world come to cover the former years' artwork with new artwork at Crush Walls. The alleys have become lit-up walkways to explore art between bars. RiNo quickly became a trendy neighborhood during its transformation. While it still is expanding east with new construction and improvements, the hottest restaurants, bars, co-working spaces, and hotels are moving in.

1

LOS CHINGONES

Chef Troy Guard serves up bold, flavorful Mexican-ish favorites with a spin. They don't claim to be authentic Mexican and they aren't Tex-Mex. **LOS CHINGONES'** menu was inspired by Guard's teen years in coastal San Diego. The flavors are, per the website, "sassy, spicy and sometimes irreverent, but always an adventure." The dishes are for sharing, like the Mexican-style shrimp cóctel: poached shrimp, rooster salsa, clamato, avocado, and chips; or the Pig Nachos: pork belly, house-made chorizo, pinto bean puree, pickled jalapeño, red onion, crema, guacamole, and pico. Bonus points to Los Chingones for complimentary chips and salsa, which seems to be a chargeable item at other competing restaurants.

TIP

ALL NIGHT LONG

Keep the night going at Los Lounge, the late-night lounge conjoined to Los Chingones that serves tacos and cocktails in a lounge setting. Reservations are not necessary. It's first come, first served seating.

If shared items aren't of interest, a platter of assorted tacos is the perfect portion. Chow down on the Baja fish tacos with the option of grilled or fried mahi mahi topped with chingon slaw, pickled onion, and chipotle aioli; the jalapeño popper taco: beer-battered, five-cheese blend, guajillo ranch, and pico; or the fried tofu taco: fajita veggies, carrot salsa, Cotija cheese, and cilantro. The quesadilla of the day is the perfect portion size for one.

The rooftop bar is my favorite spot to meet friends for cocktails. They have an extensive list of tequilas ranging from blanco to mezcal and anejo to reposado. Like any good Mexican restaurant, margaritas rule the menu but Los Chingones puts an emphasis on their cocktail classics. Sip on the Passion Fruit Paloma: tequila blanco, fresh squeezed grapefruit, lime, agave, passion fruit, and Sprite.

Feeling generous after all that food? Tell your server to add the "Buy a 6-PK for the Kitchen" to your bill as a thank you to the kitchen. The back of house will greatly appreciate the beers.

2 SUPER MEGA BIEN

Inside the Ramble Hotel sits the no-frills dim sum cart restaurant **SUPER MEGA BIEN**. This isn't a traditional Cantonese dim sum; it's an exploration of Latin American flavors presented in small plates on a pushcart. Chef Dana Rodriguez named this restaurant after the response one of her line cooks would answer with—"super mega bien"—when she asked how he was doing. Chef Rodriguez's other concept, Work & Class, is just across the street and faces Super Mega Bien. Reservations are not taken, and if you aren't there by 6 p.m., you can expect a long wait.

Once you sit, the dim sum cart greets you before you can look at the menu. This is my favorite because I can start eating immediately. The cart items are always changing from day to day so it's difficult to plan in advance. You will be given a sheet listing the dim sum cart items when

you sit. Then each time you request something off the cart, they stamp it. The sweet potato egg rolls were my favorite, and I hope they will bring them back during the harvest months.

The food from the menu is served family-style for three or more people. I used to tell people to order off the dim sum cart, but once I tried the shared plates I was hooked. Spanish Rice La Cazuela has crispy rice with roasted vegetables in a cast iron skillet, then topped with goat and manchego cheeses. Another delicious option is the Braised Lamb Mixiote: braised Colorado lamb wrapped in a banana leaf with mole negro and served with a grilled cactus salad, hot sauce, and house-made tortillas. While you're in the mood to share things, order the group cocktails like the Peruvian margarita or sangria. One drink covers about four servings.

3 STOWAWAY KITCHEN

Walking down the sidewalk of RiNo you'll find a small staircase and ramp up to **STOWAWAY KITCHEN**. On the outside it looks like a warehouse, but inside is a tiny oasis. The whitewashed walls with rugged wood floors brighten the space up. Plant vines found their home and rooted themselves across the walls. The space feels light and airy with a garage door that opens to the street.

Stowaway Kitchen is a coffee shop, but in addition to coffee, they offer an eclectic menu of globally inspired dishes. As the owners traveled around the world, they collected recipes to bring to their kitchen. The recipes are meant to nourish with comfort. For example the Colorado Colorado—salt and vinegar potato hash, kurobuta ham (or avocado), pickled radishes, asparagus, and spicy adobo sauce with poached eggs—is their best-selling dish because of how well the vegetable flavors meld together.

The kitchen is typically where people hang out when they are at each other's homes. It's the welcoming point and the place to comfort each other. Stowaway Kitchen used this idea to create their concept.

4

CALL

CALL and its sister restaurant, Beckon, are in side-by-side houses in RiNo. CALL focuses on a casual atmosphere while Beckon is a private chef experience. CALL is an all-day fast-casual restaurant where you order at the counter and wait for your order to be delivered or called. The menu is Scandinavian influenced from executive chef/culinary director Duncan Holmes's time spent working in kitchens in Denmark and Sweden. The patio is open year-round with blankets and heaters for chilly winters and umbrellas for shade in the hot summers.

The menu was originally focused on morning and lunch service to offer a true Scandinavian cafe, with mix-and-match offerings from the open counter to pair with an espresso or tonic drink, but after a year in service CALL added a dinner and happy hour service. The day menu offers a light breakfast and lunch. Items include Pork and Fried Egg Sandwich: smoked

pork, arugula, giardiniera, and aioli; Furi-Cado: avocado on the half shell, furikake (Japanese saesoning), and herbs; and Ableskiver: Danish pancake puff with preserved fruit and ricotta. The evening menu includes The Dog: Olympia Provisions frank, dog sauce, thin-sliced cucumber, and fried shallots served on a toasted house-made brioche bun; or the Potted Chicken: confit chicken, celery, fennel, aioli, and topped with rye. The mix-and-match counter includes an assortment of baked breads, pastries, desserts, and specialty offerings such as a pretzel baguette sandwich or shaved shoestring fries.

CALL is best known for its cocktails. The Share-A-Bowl is the choice of an Aperol or Campari spritz for two, served in a large bowl with two straws.

CALL was named one of America's Best New Restaurants by *Bon Appétit* in 2018. It's a perfect place for a coffee meeting or date night.

THE FIVE POINTS CRAWL

1. **BIRDCALL**, 800 E. 26th Ave., Denver, (720) 361-2976, eatbirdcall.com

2. **ROSENBERG'S BAGELS**, 725 E. 26th Ave., Denver, (720) 440-9880, rosenbergsbagels.com

3. **BEET BOX**, 1030 E. 22nd Ave., Denver, (303) 861-0017, beetboxdenver.com

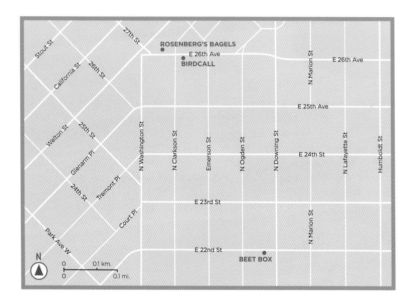

Five Points

Tastes on Point

THIS DIVERSE NEIGHBORHOOD IS ONE OF THE O.G.s of Denver's history. The Black American West Museum pays homage to the African Americans from the pioneer era who originally settled here. During the segregation era many African-American families resided here when they were pushed out of the city. It accommodated many famous blues and jazz singers when they visited town and weren't allowed to stay in the hotels where they were performing.

Five Points is home to cozy coffee shops, craft breweries, bakeries, and restaurants. You'll find soul food on every corner and after a day of eating, everyone shuffles into the live music venues like Cervantes Masterpiece. You can't find better flavors than at the establishments in Five Points.

1   BIRDCALL

I'm not clucking around—flock to **BIRDCALL** for fried chicken sandwiches! This is the newest concept from sister companies Park & Co. and Park Burger. Birdcall is bright yellow and white on the outside and hard to miss. It moved into the Five Points neighborhood and learned the importance of understanding the neighborhood. They have since changed their approach and let the communities build Birdcall.

You'll notice local muralist Mike Graves painted the walls on the inside and out. One thing all Birdcalls locations have in common are the epic patios, which provide more seating outdoors than indoors.

If this is your first time, you have to order their most popular sandwich, The Nashville Hot: crispy chicken tossed in Nashville hot or "extra hot" sauce, with sweet butter pickle chips to cool the temperature. Other favorites are The Southern Chicken: crispy chicken, pimento cheese spread, southern coleslaw; or The Deluxe: crispy chicken, buttermilk herb mayo, bacon, Pepper Jack cheese, tomato slices, and shredded lettuce.

Birdcall is an ever-evolving concept. They are disrupting the quick-service industry to improve the customer experience, improve hospitality, and continue to keep the price point low, and they have been experimenting with self-ordering kiosks and drive-thrus.

2 ROSENBERG'S BAGELS

This Jewish deli was the result of owner Joshua Pollack missing bagels when he was in college. He wanted to open a bagel store, Italian deli, and New York pizzeria, but he couldn't figure out the best way to make his bagels. He wanted them to taste like the New York–style bagels he grew up with. Joshua felt that there must have been something about the New York City water that made their bagels unique. He began his water testing and found it was the mineral content, specifically magnesium, that helps bagels turn out chewier with a soft and fluffy inside. He had perfected the perfect bagel texture. Rosenberg's uses a traditional, Old World bagel-making method that's been around for hundreds of years. Each bagel is shaped by hand, boiled, and then baked.

When you order at **ROSENBERG'S,** you can choose a signature bagel sandwich like The Standard—a bagel sandwich with gravlax, cream cheese, tomatoes, capers, and onions on an egg everything bagel. Or you can make your own sandwich. Scottish Smoked Salmon—the second most popular—is cold-smoked, which keeps it fresh and raw.

Community is everything to Rosenberg's. They emphasize supporting and giving back. In a neighborhood that's seen a lot of change, Joshua has made it a mission to hire people from the community and pays a living wage of $15 an hour.

3

BEET BOX

BEET BOX is the top bakery in Five Points, with neighbors stopping by daily for a latte or pastry. The restaurant may seem small when you walk in, but there is a walkway into the booth area that many co-work from. The walls and ceilings are covered with plants and the sounds of mixers and espresso machines fill the silence.

They offer a small selection of breakfast and lunch sandwiches with a large selection of fresh-baked pastries, doughnuts, cakes, and more. Beet Box is a scratch-to-order vegan bakery and cafe. The baked doughnuts are my favorite morning treat paired with a coffee or kombucha. I love the coconut the most, but I'm also a fan of the apple and almond. The flavorful doughnuts are dense and never crumble. They have a cake-like consistency. On the breakfast menu you can always get the Breakfast Sandwich that is fully customizable or opt for the weekly rotating flavored quiche, such as the chickpea cashew, sold by the slice. Lighter pastry options include the croissants: plain, chocolate, almond, or spinach mushroom that flake away when torn in half; dense gluten-free scones: apple cinnamon, coconut chocolate chunk, currant ginger or blackberry lavender; or the gluten-free muffins: chai spice, lemon blueberry, banana chocolate, or cherry almond.

Beet Box offers small 4-inch cakes daily. The Lemon Lavender cake is three tiers of lemon curd and lavender buttercream between the cake and topped with blueberry meringues. The lemon adds a light zest while the lavender calms the palate. If you're looking for a more decadent option, then the chocolate raspberry cake is divine with raspberry buttercream and a chocolate ganache. I once watched a man eat an entire gluten-free almond tiramisu cake for breakfast. He took about an hour to eat it, but with every bite his face beamed. I couldn't resist wanting that same feeling so I also bought a cake.

The cupcakes are glorious just like the daily cakes. The flavors are always unique aside from the chocolate and vanilla, like the vanilla strawberry, chocolate raspberry, or almond chocolate. Take a dozen home because

once you try one, you will want all the flavors. Other sweet treats include the bars: beet brownie, gluten-free turtle brownies, butterscotch blondies, and gluten free s'mores; and the sweet tarts: almond and seasonal fruit, gluten-free key lime, and gluten-free seasonal flavor.

Beet Box is a great choice for lunch. Either take a loaf of bread to-go and make a sandwich at home or try one from the menu. The must-try sandwich is the Tofu Banh Mi: crispy baked tofu, pickled vegetables, housemade vegan mayo, cucumber, cilantro, and lime on a fresh-baked baguette. Another popular offering is the Chickpea of the Sea: chickpea salad with parsley, dill, kalamata olives, tomatoes, house-made vegan mayo, cucumber, and butter lettuce on multigrain bread. It's the perfect taste of the Mediterranean.

THE UPTOWN CRAWL

1. **PARK & CO.**, **439 E. 17th Ave.**, Denver, (720) 328-6732, parkandcodenver.com

2. **STEUBEN'S**, **523 E. 17th Ave.**, Denver, (303) 830-1001, steubens.com

3. **MARCZYK FINE FOODS**, **770 E. 17th Ave.**, Denver, (303) 894-9499, marczyk.com

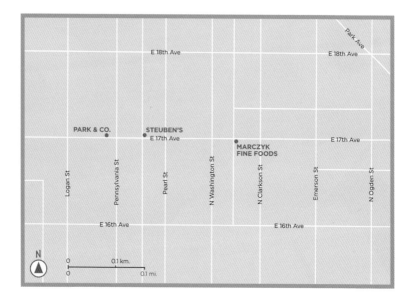

Uptown

The Happiest Hours and Upbeat Patios

WELCOME TO RESTAURANT ROW! Seventeenth Avenue is lined with eateries that offer a taste of everything: burgers, tacos, sandwiches, pho, steak, vegan-friendly, and more. Weaving between the restaurant establishments are upscale condos and Victorian homes. It's a clash of old and new that makes this neighborhood one of the most sought after to live in. Trendy Uptown is always bustling with people hopping from restaurant to restaurant. Early happy hours attract the business crowd rushing out of work as early as 3 p.m. on a Monday to maximize their intake of cheap eats and cold drinks. Uptown is the perfect area to gather with friends before hitting the town or to enjoy the best brunch options per capita.

1

PARK & CO.

There is nothing basic about the burgers at **PARK & CO.** Their sister concept, Park Burger, paved the way for Denver's burger scene, and the owners introduced Park & Co. as a spinoff concept in the Uptown neighborhood. Park & Co.'s menu includes burgers, sandwiches, and salads. Indulge in the Au Poivre Burger: peppercorn crusted patty, caramelized onions, brie cheese, arugula, and a spread of béarnaise aioli; or heat your mouth with the Chilango Burger: beef patty, guacamole, cheddar cheese, and fresh-cut jalapeños. All burgers are served with lettuce, tomato, onion, pickle, and an Aspen Bakery

potato bun. Upgrade the burger patty to a grilled chicken, buffalo, or veggie patty. The buffalo patty best accompanies the barbecue burger: cheddar cheese, crispy onions, and barbecue sauce. While gluten-free buns are available, the burgers are also still delicious served on a bed of lettuce.

The sandwiches are shockingly savory. The Fuego Steak Melt with shaved ribeye, jalapeño, tomato, Pepper Jack cheese, and chipotle aioli is the start to the sandwich offerings. The menu includes the tofu po' boy: beer-battered tofu, shredded lettuce, tomatoes, and béarnaise aioli; Park french dip made with roasted NY strip; buffalo chicken sandwich; and more.

Regardless of whether you are eating the sandwich or the burger, the hardest decision is which fries to order. Park & Co. offers hand-cut french fries or sweet potato fries, but the admirable options are truffle and parmesan, cajun, or the works: cheese sauce, ranch, bacon, and scallions. Or go big by ordering the stuffed tater tots from the appetizer menu: jalapeños, bacon, sour cream, cheddar, and scallions with ranch dressing and cheese sauce to dip.

Happy hour takes place 7 days a week with varying times but the same menu. The Park Burger Sliders are only $2. The Uptown Nachos with red chili pork, chipotle aioli, pickled onions, jalapeños, nacho cheese, tomatoes, lettuce, sour cream, and guacamole heap over the plate for $7 or $14 when it is not happy hour.

2

STEUBEN'S

Transport to the 1960s with diner-esque ambience at **STEUBEN'S**. The restaurant is decorated with powder-blue tables, shiny brown retro barstools, and stainless steel accents. The dessert case is eye catching with cakes, hand-spun milkshakes, cookies, ice cream sundaes, Italian sodas, and throwback candies.

Steuben's serves American comfort food with a modern twist. Every order should start with deviled eggs and chicken-fried pickles. The extensive menu is updated frequently but a few staples are always available. The Steuben's burger: a brioche bun with lettuce, onion, tomato, mayo, and mustard; the Nashville hot fried chicken: spicy bacon, brown sugar–glazed chicken, Texas toast, pickles, and mashed potatoes; and Joe's

TIP

STACK THOSE DOLLAR, DOLLAR BILLS Y'ALL!

Sundays are for the queens. Make a reservation in advance and let the drag queens serenade you while sipping on bottomless mimosas.

breakfast served all day: two eggs any style, crispy smashed potatoes, toast, and choice of breakfast meat.

While lunch and dinner are busy, the crowds flock to Steuben's for weekend brunch. The early bird gets the worm while later diners can expect an hour wait. The bacon, egg, and cheese sandwich is so delicious it's available all day. The brioche bun tenderly collapses while the egg yolk breaks between the teeth and the thick-cut bacon and American cheese add to the overall chewiness. Other brunch items include the smothered breakfast burrito, chicken and waffles, huevos rancheros, and avocado goddess toast.

Late-night cravings can be cured at the walk-up take-out counter. It has its own entrance off 17th Avenue. Steuben's offers a select menu of the most popular late-night munchies like hot dogs, Philly cheesesteaks, and Steubie Snacks: deep-fried braised pork shoulder rolled in powdered sugar.

3

MARCZYK FINE FOODS

Locals skip the grocery chains and shop at **MARCZYK'S** for a curated experience of produce, meats, wine, and non-perishables. Everything you could possibly need is under one roof. Not only is it a market, but there is also a fine wine shop attached selling wines that are just right for drinking at that moment. That means there isn't a cellar with high-priced vintage wines. Instead the shelves and wine racks house mostly $15 and under wines. They make it affordable to taste your way through their whole wine selection.

If there is one thing Marczyk is famous in Denver for, it's their sandwiches. They are fresh to order from the deli with warm baked bread from the bakery and fresh-sliced meat from the butcher. Don't wait for Thanksgiving for that turkey dinner. Order the Colonial Turkey: roasted turkey breast, cranberry sauce, brie, and local lettuce on toasted Marczyk white levain. Get saucy with The Cackalacky: Niman Ranch smoked pulled pork, Carolina gold barbecue sauce, and coleslaw on a brioche bun. Skip the trip to Alaska and order The Alaskan: market-made smoked salmon spread,

bacon, and arugula on toasted Marczyk white levain. While the sandwich menu is lengthy, there's always a sandwich of the day to help make up your mind.

Once you pick a sandwich you can shop the aisles for the perfect side, whether it's a pasta salad or a bag of potato chips. The coolers by the checkout have an array of drinks from kombucha to cold brew to sparkling sodas. Loop back to the deli for your completed sandwich and then check out at the register. If you have a loyalty card, they will pick up your sandwich tab after each membership milestone.

Enjoy your elevated sandwich on the picnic tables outside by the parking lot. Watch the chaos of 17th Avenue pass by as you sink your teeth into that warm, soft bread. Eating a sandwich from Marczyk's is almost a rite of passage to being a true Denverite.

Another perk of Marczyk's is the Prepared Food section with ready-to-eat meals to grab on your way home. It's just as good as a homemade meal, except you didn't have to do all the prep or clean up. Some of the items are old family recipes, which is why they taste so nostalgic, like Pete's Mom's Potato Salad or Mamie's Mac and Cheese. You can even pick up dessert. Marczyk Bros. Ice Cream is available next to the register, which couldn't be more perfect product placement. It's creamy and made fresh from Morning Fresh milk and cream. The flavors rotate based on the season and demand.

After you've experienced Marczyk Fine Foods at its finest, you can send them an inquiry for their party catering. They offer just about everything they have in store as a catering platter or individual lunches.

THE CAPITOL HILL CRAWL

1. **CUBA CUBA CAFE & BAR**, 1173 Delaware St., Denver, (720) 328-6732, cubacubacafe.com

2. **SASSAFRAS AMERICAN EATERY**, 320 E. Colfax Ave., Denver, (303) 831-6233, sassafrasamericaneatery.com

3. **PUB ON PENN**, 1278 Pennsylvania St., Denver, (303) 861-8638

4. **HUDSON HILL**, 619 E. 13th Ave., Denver, (303) 832-0776, hudsonhilldenver.com

5. **SNARF'S SANDWICHES**, 1001 E. 11th Ave., Denver, (303) 832-9999, eatsnarfs.com

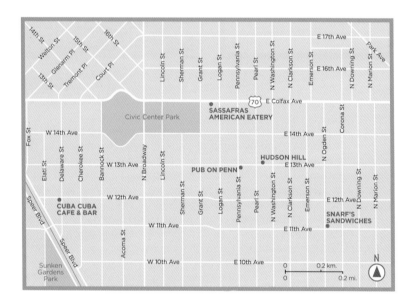

Capitol Hill

The Politics of Partying

HISTORY AND SWAGGER STRANGELY GO TOGETHER on the streets of Capitol Hill. Large mansions, Victorian homes, and funky apartment buildings from the '70s and '80s line this neighborhood all the way to the gold-domed Colorado State Capitol. You can find iconic spots like the Molly Brown House Museum and The Church Nightclub. Running through Cap Hill is the infamous Colfax Avenue. Playboy's Hugh Hefner dubbed it to be the "Longest, Wickedest Street in America." It still lives up to that name today. It has the best party scene, local art, funky boutiques, and eclectic restaurants. Finding parking in Cap Hill is next to impossible since very few apartment buildings have parking spots. The one-way streets keep traffic flowing, but the best way to get around is by foot, bike, or scooter. In the daytime you can find everyone picnicking and playing Frisbee at Cheesman Park. A night on the town isn't complete without karaoke at Armida's, piano singalongs at Charlie Brown's, dancing with a mini pitcher of beer in hand at Charlie's—an LGBTQ-friendly bar that welcomes everyone—and a late-night bite at Sexy Pizza. It was hard to narrow down the Cap Hill restaurants to one crawl because there are so many great places.

1

CUBA CUBA CAFE & BAR

Come find that piece of your heart that desires the Latin music, sun-soaked terrace, and tropical food at **CUBA CUBA**. This restaurant is one of Denver's best kept secrets and once you visit, you will know why. The sidewalk is lined with banana leaf trees and tropical foliage. Step inside this Cuban oasis and prepare your heart to never want to leave. The walls are aqua with bright murals, and the bar is draped in a large rum selection. Locals love to exchange stories while counting the number of mojito pitchers that go out.

The old wooden floors creak as you pass by into the other dining rooms. My preferred spot is on the enclosed patio. It's a glass house on the front with doors that create an open-air environment. The sun bakes through

the windows and gives a warm, summer feel. Off of the enclosed patio are two small outdoor patios.

The ambience of Cuba Cuba will transport you to Havana, but it's the food that will blow your mind. Many of the recipes come from American-Cuban owner Kristy Bigelow's grandmother. A few of her favorites are the *vaca frita* (mojo marinated flank steak seared and topped with sautéed onions) and the *picadillo al caballo* (ground beef, potatoes, olives, and peppers, topped with a fried egg).

I recommend starting with the Mariquitas Cubana. Request a pitcher of the blackberry mojito made with fresh mint and real sugarcane. Then order the three types of empanadas: *ropa vieja*, *hongo*, and *picadillo*. Unbutton your pants button and dive in to the entrees like the Ropa Vieja de Casa or the Churrasco con Chimichurri.

If you can find room to fancy yourself with dessert then do it. The traditional flan is a favorite, but venture out to the tres leches topped with meringue and caramel candy. Dessert is never complete without a coffee, so add on the cafe con leche or the *cortadito*.

2 SASSAFRAS AMERICAN EATERY

I love Sassafras because it doesn't need to be the weekend to enjoy brunch. Every day is brunch here and you don't need to be sassy to devour the southern-inspired food. **SASSAFRAS** was the brainchild of proprietress Julia Grother. She put up an ad for a chef specializing in southern cuisine and received more than 70 applicants. Along came chef Colin Mallet of Louisiana with an entire tasting that blew Grother away. The two of them and their other partner, Richard Stewart, opened Sassafras in 2012.

The restaurant is decorated with collectors' spoons, cross-stitched signs, pigs, roosters, wood hutches filled with adorable teacups, and a large "Welcome Home" pennant sign. The southern charm and welcoming tone immediately make you feel at home. The menu has approachable classic southern dishes like biscuits and gravy, but Grother wanted to give customers an experience and encourage them to venture out with exciting entrees.

Sassafras wood is used to cook everything here, hence the name of the restaurant. The boozy milkshakes were made famous with coverage from Thrillist, Paula Deen, and USA Today. The Cap'n Crunch and Cinnamon Toast Crunch milkshakes are staples while the other flavors are changing. The shakes are served in tall glasses and topped with whipped cream. Once you taste the beignets and berry jams, you will crave for a Sassafras location to open near you. Luckily you can take home the jams from the retail area next to the host stand. The berry jam is made sweet with just a touch of cinnamon while the voodoo jam is heated by bell peppers and jalapeño.

The signature and most Instagrammable dish is Chicken-Fried Egg and Buffalo Hash: free-range buffalo smoked on pecan wood, jalapeño cornbread, and Fresno chile hollandaise. The buffalo hash is put into a ring

The mini Marys are the way to go. The flight includes your choice of 4 Bloody Marys out of 8.

mold on the flat top, while the cornbread is toasted on the griddle. They don't allow substitutions because it's a dish you can't get anywhere else. They want you to experience it as it was meant to be.

Sassafras serves the lunch menu all day. The popular mac and cheese is rich and creamy, made with Tillamook sharp cheddar. The fan favorites are the blackened chicken mac and barbecue mac made with pulled pork and collard greens. The green tomato po' boys explode with flavor: crispy cornmeal-crusted green tomatoes, arugula, goat cheese, sun-dried tomatoes, and sun-dried tomato vinaigrette. Don't skip dessert!

3

PUB ON PENN

PUB ON PENN is the definition of a neighborhood bar in Cap Hill. The emerald-green walls are met by old brick, the neon drink signs give the bar ample lighting, and it is packed with neighborhood regulars. The weekly food and drink specials can't be beat. You can get tacos and a beer for under $5 on Monday, $1 pulled pork, chorizo, or beef sliders on Friday, or $4 breakfast burritos on the weekends. The Wednesday night wing special is what calls me and my friends in. All you can eat wings for $8 and a $9 pitcher of beer to wash it down might be the best deal ever. The wings are saucy, juicy, and crispy. They come by the dozen or half-dozen and the sauces vary from hot to barbecue. Another hot night to visit is during Thursday's $4 burger special. After a long day of work nothing sounds better than a big burger. You'll need two hands to hold onto it. Add a side of fries and call it good. I should mention, burger night coincidentally falls on team trivia night, so arrive early.

Pub on Penn captures a crowd at any time of day because they offer daytime specials until 3 p.m. The shuffleboard darts and pool are hard to jump in on because people love to host impromptu tournaments between their friends. If you can't play a bar game or find a seat, you can hang on the patio. It might feel like walking out of a Vegas casino because the sun shines so bright after being inside the dark bar.

4 HUDSON HILL

Hipsters unite! This coffee shop and coworking space during the day quickly turns into a craft cocktail bar in the late afternoon. Many Denverites only work until about 3 p.m., and then everyone can be found at a happy hour starting around 4 p.m. **HUDSON HILL** is the best happy hour spot for Cap Hill. It doesn't get much better than $5 well drinks or a $4 "khores" lager paired with an $8 grilled cheese. The happy hour menu also includes an $8 bartender's choice cocktail special.

Hudson Hill is a mixture of romance and hip. Music crackles from the record player, oversized U-shaped leather bench seats line the brick walls, and the dim lighting adds a sophisticated elegance. The staff is enthusiastic about their drinks and music. They know everyone that walks in as well as their drink of choice.

I prefer to sit at the bar because the barstools are drilled to the floor and give you a perfect personal space bubble. It's great to set up shop with a laptop and latte or keep your distance on an awkward first date. My favorite sips are the Lady Jane: bourbon, ginger, lemon, carpano antica, and fresh mint; and the Green Hour: tequila, coconut, mint, bitter orange, and a dash of nutmeg. The food offerings are slim and more for snacking. The heartiest option aside from the grilled cheese is the cheese platter. You can also get spicy pickled okra, a fresh baguette with French butter, or warm chocolate chip cookies.

5

SNARF'S SANDWICHES

When asked where to get the best sandwich in Denver, I tell people to head to **SNARF'S**. Snarf's came about when "Snarf" Jimmy Seidel was on a quest to find the world's finest sandwich. He has now grown SNARF's to over 20 restaurants in three states.

There is so much to love about SNARF's, from their strange tile mosaics and brightly colored shops to the gooey desserts and oven-toasted bread. Sure, it's a sandwich shop, but it's a craveable sandwich shop. They put all their love into every made-to-order, award-winning sandwich. Premium meats range from prime rib and smoked brisket to rotisserie chicken and New York steak. They have the standard toppings like mayo, mustard, hot peppers, onions, lettuce, tomato, and pickles, but you can also add mushrooms, artichokes, avocado, sprouts, and bacon.

There are three different sandwich sizes: Novice (5 inches), SNARF's (7 inches), and Pro (12 inches). My go-to sandwiches are the french dip with cheesy swiss and provolone served au jus or the turkey and provolone cheese sandwich with extra pickles.

SNARF's has fresh romaine and red leaf lettuce salads too. The cobb salad is a great choice with avocado, American and provolone cheese, tomato, onion, hard-boiled egg, and chopped bacon served with a toasted slice of bread. They also offer options for kids: grilled cheese, peanut butter and jelly, hot dog, or peanut butter, banana, and honey sandwiches.

TIP

Want to Know a Secret? There's a "SNARF's not on the menu" menu with nine specialty creations. You can find it hidden on their website. Try the German Dog: Hebrew National all-beef frank with bacon, swiss, mayo, mustard, horseradish, sauerkraut, onion, pickle, tomato, and hot peppers.

THE GOVERNORS PARK CRAWL

1. **PIZZERIA LOCALE**, 550 Broadway, Denver, (720) 508-8828, pizzerialocale.com

2. **VESPER LOUNGE**, 233 E. 7th Ave., Denver, (720) 328-0314, vesperdenver.com

3. **PABLO'S COFFEE**, 630 E. 6th Ave., Denver, (303) 744-3323, pabloscoffee.com

4. **FRUITION RESTAURANT**, 1313 E. 6th Ave., Denver, (303) 831-1962, fruitionrestaurant.com

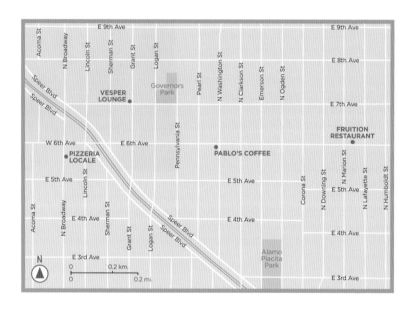

Governors Park

Mansions and Dive Bars

GOVERNORS PARK IS A QUIET, WALKABLE NEIGHBORHOOD next to bustling Capitol Hill and South Broadway. The park itself is surrounded by the Governor's Residence at the Boettcher Mansion, Malo Mansion, and Grant-Humphreys Mansion. High-rise apartment buildings and restaurants fill the gaps in between the micro-mansions. Finding a parking spot in this dense neighborhood can seem impossible, but if you park far you will likely run into several dogs to pet. Almost every resident has a dog here.

This trendy neighborhood has three dive bars including Vesper Lounge, several fast-casual concepts like Pizzeria Locale, and one of the top-rated restaurants in the city, Fruition Restaurant. In 2014 the most exciting thing to happen was the addition of a Trader Joe's. Since then, Governors Park has doubled in residents and hip, new apartments have been constructed.

1

PIZZERIA LOCALE

On the corner of Broadway and 6th stands **PIZZERIA LOCALE**, serving fast-fired Neapolitan-style pizza. It re-creates the flavors and vibe of an Italian pizzeria in Naples, Italy, that founders Lachlan Mackinnon-Patterson and Bobby Stuckey love. It started as a restaurant in 2011 with table service in Boulder and turned into a fast-casual version upon opening its doors in Denver in 2013. They drew in a wider range of people with fast food prices while still giving personalized hospitality experiences.

Pizzeria Locale's ingredients are domestic by design, meaning they are thoughtfully sourced and of the highest quality, similar to what you could import from Italy. This not only supports local purveyors, but also helps reduce the restaurant's carbon footprint. Pizza isn't the only thing they slice; front and center by the pizza oven is a beautiful shiny red hand-cranked prosciutto meat slicer. Ask to sample a fresh slice of meat or go all in and order the Prosciutto & Arugula red pizza: La Quercia Prosciutto Americano, red pizza sauce, mozzarella, and arugula.

The details are in the ingredients with each ingredient weighed and batched to assure consistency. Fresh vegetables are chopped every day and roasted in the oven. They are seasoned with olive oil, salt, and pepper. The pizza sauce is a thick mixture of tomatoes to ensure they release the best flavors when cooked in the oven. This is a twist on the Neopolitan way that serves uncooked tomatoes. They are tiny, vibrant, and acidic, which gives the pizza a tangy flavor. The best way to taste the pizza sauce is to order the Margherita pizza: mozzarella and basil. It's simple but offers a taste of each ingredient.

Pizzeria Locale also serves salads like the Caponata: mixed greens, eggplant, zucchini, red onions, red peppers, black olives, parmesan, and house-made red wine vinaigrette. The Antica salad is my favorite to split as a side with my pizza. It's a simple salad of mixed greens, grape tomatoes, parmesan, and red wine vinaigrette.

If you're looking for a sweeter option, order the Nutella Pizza: chewy pizza dough drizzled with Nutella and dusted with powdered sugar. There is also the Bundino, a layered butterscotch pudding with a layer of melted chocolate ganache and topped with house-made whipped cream. They are mini in size and mighty in flavor.

2 VESPER LOUNGE

When the sun sets, all the locals flock to **VESPER LOUNGE**. This neighborhood watering hole is where the bartender knows your name, the jukebox is rocking, and the cocktails are flowing. All hail the Vesper cocktail, James Bond's signature drink: London Dry Gin, Skyy Vodka, Lillet Blanc infused with lemon peel, and Grains of Paradise.

Vesper pours eight cocktails on tap daily: Old Fashioned, Dark & Stormy, Aperol Spritz, Paloma, Silver Gin Fizz, Hawaiian John Daily, and Moscow Mule. Each cocktail is made with top-shelf liquors that won't give a hangover unless you over-indulge. At $6 a cocktail it's hard to tab out and go home. Good thing chef/owner Frank Bonanno created a drool-worthy Mediterranean bar menu at affordable prices.

Moroccan bar nuts, artichokes, and wings are labeled on the menu as Snacks for Drinkers. I love the wings so much that I have licked the bones dry. Trust me, you will do the same. The trio of dips served with warm pita are perfect for a light bite or to accompany your meal. My top three choices are the red pepper hummus, pesto, and baba ghanoush. The other dips are olive and tzatziki.

The menu nods to the late comedian John Belushi and his famous *SNL* (*Saturday Night Live*) skit with the title "Cheeseburger! Cheeseburger! Cheeseburger!" and an outline of his face across the top. The Sunday special is a cheeseburger and a draft beer for $10. Any day but Sunday, the Greek burger is my favorite: a beef patty topped with feta, fattoush, tzatziki, olive tapenade, and gyro meat. All burgers are served with fries.

If a burger isn't in the cards, order one of the pitas. The gyro with feta, fattoush, and tzatziki is a traditional choice; or you can mix it up with Colorado shaved lamb with tzatziki, feta, fattoush, and lettuce; or spicy chicken with honey garlic sauce, saganaki, and lettuce.

Vesper is a staple in the Governors Park neighborhood. It's a no-frills atmosphere that attracts all walks of life.

3 PABLO'S COFFEE

This is not a coffee shop for setting up your computer and aimlessly scrolling the internet while sipping a latte; it's a coffee shop for human interaction. It's a place to explore. You'll notice the free stickers and signs that say "No Wi-Fi, Free Hugs." This may put off a newcomer, but the regulars appreciate the no wi-fi rule.

PABLO'S COFFEE will celebrate its 25th anniversary in 2020. Founder Craig Conner opened the coffee shop after leaving his corporate job. He created one of the first craft coffee roasters in Denver. They source the best coffee beans from around the world and roast them using sustainable practices. They specialize in exotic single-origin coffees as well as funky blends like Danger Monkey. Every roast is focused on delivering the best-tasting balance, body, and sweetness.

The baristas take pride in their skills of making unique latte art or sharing the roastery techniques for the coffee they just poured. They likely know your name and your preferred order. Pablo's is my favorite spot to grab an iced coffee and M&M cookie on the patio.

Walking into Pablo's on 6th Avenue and Washington is like stepping into a time machine. The ceiling is checkered black and white with retro red barstools at the high-top tables; the natural wood colored low-top tables and chairs are banged up and dented with character; jungle vibes come from the live plants in the front windows; the lounge area puts off the grandparent vibe but without the plastic covers over the green suede chairs. The space is complex with variety for a reason: to welcome a variety of people.

4 FRUITION RESTAURANT

FRUITION RESTAURANT is the brainchild of James Beard Award–winning chef Alex Seidel. It is and always will be his baby. Though Seidel never imagined owning a restaurant, he is most thankful for Fruition as they move past their 10th anniversary and look forward to another decade.

Seidel periodically changes the menu to stay fresh and current on food in season. It's a small neighborhood restaurant with an intimate ambience, open for dinner service only. The cherry wood chairs and tables are pre-set with water glasses, napkins, and silverware. The lights are dimmed low and the dining room feels light and airy. Pair all of this with impeccable service and you will find yourself returning frequently for your next meal.

Seidel serves an interpretation of sophisticated comfort food. His dishes are beautiful and photo worthy. Once you taste the food you will taste the heart and soul behind Fruition. Chef de cuisine John Lavelle is the secret to Fruition's dishes. He is always looking for inspiration to create new dishes. Trends do not determine the menu because they become irrelevant over time. Fruition is not about just the plate and food presentation; it is about the ingredients and the people behind them. Though they create new menus constantly, there are a few favorites that are always available: the French onion soup, pork belly carbonara, and potato-wrapped oysters Rockefeller. As for the rest of the menu at Fruition, it is best to check the website for the latest offerings. A few items from the past that really caught my attention are the tender Maple Leaf Farms Duck with

heirloom beets, frisée, palisade cherry mostarda, and foie jus; the juicy Bavette Steak Caesar salad with grilled little gem lettuce, fingerlings, and cauliflower and black garlic purée; and the po' boy with sweetbreads, fennel, and mustard seed.

THE CITY PARK CRAWL

1. **TRIPLE TREE CAFÉ**, 1201 E. Colfax Ave. #102, Denver, (720) 917-1000, tripletreecafe.com

2. **PETE'S KITCHEN**, 1962 E. Colfax Ave., Denver, (303) 321-31039, petesrestaurant.com

3. **TACOS, TEQUILA, WHISKEY**, 1514 York St., Denver, (720) 475-1337, tacostequilawhiskey.com

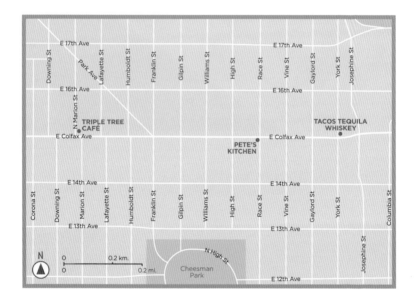

City Park

Retro Eateries

CITY PARK WAS THE FIRST PARK OUTSIDE of the original Denver outskirts, but as the city grew it filled in its way to the park. Now it's part of history with East High School being the first high school in Denver and longtime legend Pete Contos helping build the restaurant scene down East Colfax. Named America's longest street, East Colfax is a fun street to pop in and out of different bars, grab a doughnut, experience food from different cultures, and make your way toward the park for Sunday night jazz.

1

TRIPLE TREE CAFÉ

Coffee shop by day, motorcycle gang hangout by night, **TRIPLE TREE CAFÉ** is a daytime cafe with motorcycle accents throughout. There's a large bike mural on the wall and a display of helmets at the cash register. They aren't an exclusive motorcycle cafe; they're inclusive and encourage people to ride with them.

Start your day with the Day Trip Skillet: tender mixed greens sautéed in olive oil, topped with two eggs any style and a side of hand-cut roasted potatoes; or the breakfast sandwich: choice of meat with two eggs any style topped with cheddar cheese on toasted ciabatta bread. I love the hand-cut roasted potatoes. They're topped with tomatoes, red onions, and feta cheese. They're extra crispy too. You can't start your day without a proper espresso drink. Order a *cortado* or cappuccino to sip on with your meal.

If you're arriving for lunch, Triple Tree Café has an assortment of salads and sandwiches to help fuel you through the day. The Daily Grind is savory with ham and salami layered atop juicy tomato slices, topped with provolone cheese and a savory balsamic pesto sauce. It's served with chips and pickle too.

The best time to visit is for small plates during happy hour. The beet and burrata bowl is enough for two people to share. It's sweet beets, burrata cheese, pickled red onions, and a drizzle of balsamic glaze, served with pita bread wedges. The other great choice for a heartier meal is Ridin' Solo Pizza: personal pizza made with delicious flatbread and topped with pesto, mozzarella, roasted balsamic tomatoes, and pickled red onions. Did I mention you can order wine and cocktails during happy hour too?

2

PETE'S KITCHEN

PETE'S KITCHEN is a 24-hour diner with its own bouncer to keep order when the late-night crowd stops by before they head to bed. It's humorous to think that a diner needs someone to count people going in and out, while also making sure people stay in their assigned seats. As someone who has been there at 2 a.m., it makes sense. Everyone knows each other and hops from table to table for quick conversations, but this ultimately breaks up the flow of service for the line of people waiting outside.

Pete's Kitchen is one of the many restaurants that was owned by Pete Contos. When he immigrated to Colorado in 1956, he worked hard through the industry. He was a man with a dream who started as a busboy and passed away as a local legend who helped shape the Denver food scene. Pete was even inducted into the Foodservice Hall of Fame. For over 30 years, Pete's Kitchen has been selling gyros, kabobs, and stacks of pancakes.

The specialties on the breakfast menu include the Pita Breakfast Sandwich with scrambled eggs, bacon, ham, or sausage in a pita with hash browns; Chef's Special with two pancakes, two eggs, gyro or breakfast meat, and hash browns; or the classic biscuits and gravy. Whether it's 2 a.m. or 10 a.m., all these items are tasty.

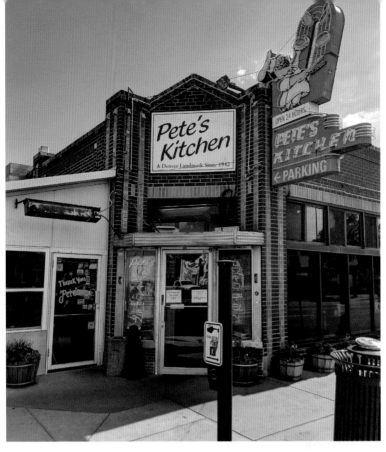

3 TACOS, TEQUILA, WHISKEY

The name says it all. This small restaurant has a community table and a few 2- or 4-person tables. The menu is handed to you with a dry erase pen because all they serve are street tacos. That means there aren't burritos, enchiladas, or tortas. There are starters though. The Queso Fundido con Chorizo is served smoking hot in a skillet. The melted Pepper Jack cheese and chorizo sizzle loudly as it is placed on your table with a brown bag of fresh-made tortilla chips. There is also Repollo Tiernos or "Little Cabbage": fried brussels sprouts, lime, spicy homemade seasoning, and Cotija cheese.

When you're ready to dive into your taco order, I suggest choosing three and possibly four. The tacos are served individually so you can mix and match. I love the Fish 'N' Beer: chipotle and beer-battered fish, slaw, pineapple guacamole, and pickled red onions. The fish is crispy with a soft crunch. The Honogs taco has grilled shiitake, crimini, and oyster mushrooms; griddled Cotija cheese; creamed cilantro corn; and ancho chile crema. When you bite into this, you're going to fall in love with mushrooms all over again.

TTW has two additional locations in Denver: one in the West Highland and the other in Governors Park. You can expect the same menu and great-tasting food at all three restaurants.

THE CONGRESS PARK CRAWL

1. **12@MADISON**, 1160 Madison St., Denver, (720) 216-0190, 12atmadison.com

2. **SWEET COOIE'S**, 3506 12th Ave., Denver, (720) 550-7140, sweetcooies.com

3. **DAE GEE KOREAN BBQ**, 827 Colorado Blvd., Denver, (720) 639-9986, daegee.com

4. **LA FILLETTE**, 4416 E. 8th Ave., Denver, (303) 355-0022, lafillettedenver.com

Congress Park

Eat in a Resident's Backyard

CUTE AS A BUTTON, CONGRESS PARK IS FILLED with little bungalow homes, the botanic garden, and large green spaces. The sidewalks are filled with squirrels sprinting tree to tree, dogs chasing after them, and lemonade stands on the corners. This neighborhood was often blurred into its surroundings, better-known neighborhoods like Capitol Hill and Cherry Creek. That was until a few restaurants moved in and elevated the dining scene. Now Congress Park has made a name for itself. With little to no real estate to expand the neighborhood, restaurants back into neighboring yards and create a more intimate dining experience that feels like dining at home. Park your car and enjoy a stroll or bike ride down the few short blocks of uneven and crooked sidewalks that give this neighborhood so much charm.

1

12@MADISON

Chef-restaurateur Jeff Osaka opened **12@MADISON** in the Congress Park neighborhood with a seasonally driven, yet approachable menu of small plates. The menu is dictated by the weather and growing seasons, which helps restaurant patrons understand the hardships that may cause an item to be unavailable for a period of time while introducing them to new tastes. It's a venture out of your comfort zone. The best challenge of this approach to cooking is that it gives the 12@Madison team the creativity to explore different flavors and make the best dishes.

The top of every menu states "We designed our menu so that all plates are meant to be shared. Whether you're dining among friends or strangers, we hope your time with us generates thoughtful conversations, brings light to your evening and leaves you with an unforgettable memory. . . ."

At 12@Madison the food speaks for itself while showing its simplicity. On a previous menu the grilled romaine was perfectly charred without being wilted and had an oven-dried tomato / red onion vinaigrette with pecorino and croutons to accompany it. It was the perfect take on something so simple but elevated to tease your taste buds. One of my favorite dishes is the salt-cured salmon with crème fraîche, scallions, and a sprinkle of everything bagel spice. It is salty, creamy, and savory, a full umami sense in every bite.

Brunch is served on Sunday with a rotating menu. The one starter that will always remain: the basket of freshly baked bite-size pastries, the sweetest start to the day. If there is a hash available on the menu, this is always a fan favorite. It is served with a protein of the day like bacon, poached eggs, and a *piperade* sauce.

You can visit Jeff Osaka's other restaurant concepts throughout Denver: Sushi-Rama is fresh and full-service sushi served on a conveyor belt; Osaka Ramen is a traditional and nontraditional ramen shop; and Tammen's Fish Market is a full-service fish market.

While the plates are thoughtfully curated, so is the decor of 12@Madison with its warm interior. The natural tones and light colors create a warm and inviting environment. The pillows on each bench make it feel snug and are there when you need to lean for a quick rest between entrees. The open kitchen concept welcomes everyone to take part in how the dishes are prepared. The highly desired chefs bar is the best spot in this 50-seat restaurant to sit and watch the craft that goes into each plate. For a more intimate evening there is a back bar, or you can enjoy the summer breeze on the patio. I love sitting on the patio with a French press to start the morning.

2 SWEET COOIE'S

Tiffany blue turquoise with accents of gold trim, light fixtures, and wallpaper will catch your eye when you enter **SWEET COOIE'S**. The interior is nothing short of exquisite. The smell of sweet candies, pastries, cookies, and ice cream will catch your attention toward the front where you will be greeted by staff wearing their vintage-inspired clothing: pressed white shirts with red and pink bowties, sana caps, and aprons. The blue and gold hutch has an entire row of glass jars filled with all the best ice cream toppings like sprinkles, nuts, and cookie crumbles. There are also pastel-colored gumballs in decorative vases extending to the ceiling. The marble countertops house a waffle iron for fresh-made waffle cones and bowls. The waffle cones are the sweetest with flavors like cookies and cream and Heath bar, accompanied by chocolate jimmies or hand-spun cotton candy.

Sweet Cooie's is named after Elaine Tamburello, the mother of owner Paul Tamburello, for her sweet cooing sounds when she soothed her children. His first concept, Little Man, was named after his father and it only felt appropriate to have his mother's influences on his next concept. Classic confectionery treats are all made from scratch, and most importantly the scoop for scoop initiative focuses on empowering females. "We will donate a portion of every scoop of ice cream we sell at Cooie's to support women's education here and around the world."

The old fashioned confectionery serves up a selection of Little Man ice cream flavors like lemon meringue pie, vegan horchata, and the infamous salted Oreo, but there are some flavors unique to just Sweet Cooie's such as the Purple Cow and Holy Cannoli. You can order a milkshake or old-fashioned sundae each topped with a maraschino cherry or the imported pecan and vanilla Scottish toffee. There is something sweet for everyone.

If the blue wavy benches are filled in the back, you can bask in the summer air on the front patio lined with red chairs and blue-striped umbrellas. Some kids even opt to sit on the street curb while their heaping ice cream cones slowly melt down their hands. Does it get any more summer than this?

LOOKING FOR THAT INSTAGRAMMABLE PIC?

Order the Gooey Cooie—their signature dish—an ice cream–filled brioche doughnut split in half and filled with your choice of ice cream. It's then warmed on a panini press and topped with a sweet sticky glaze.

3

DAE GEE KOREAN BBQ

Everyone loves **DAE GEE** because of its approachable menu that infuses traditional Korean dishes with something Americans know too well: bottomless barbecue. Don't think saucy Kansas City barbecue; it's just the name of the grill built into the table for grilling the savory meats. Dae Gee translates to pig in Korean, so what better way to "pig out." If everyone at your table is attracted to the unlimited barbecue, then stop there and order. The dinner price of $24 per person includes unlimited *galbee*—Korean for beef short ribs—which is by far the best meat. The lunch special offered Monday through Friday until 3 p.m. is $18 per person and doesn't include the galbee.

As your grill heats up, the staff will bring out a variety of side dishes including napa cabbage kimchi, cucumber kimchi, potato salad, fish cakes with vegetables, pickled yellow Korean radish, fermented onions and jalapeños, and kimchi jun. Next you will want to designate a head griller and hand them the tongs. Then get your camera ready because a platter of raw meats will be placed in front of you: *sam gyeob sal* (pork belly), *dae gee bulgogi* (pork), *sogogi bulgogi* (ribeye beef), *dak bulgogi* (chicken), and *chadol* (beef brisket). Most of the meats are thin sliced and will be ready to come off the grill in under 5 minutes. The meats are savory and go perfectly with all the side dishes.

If you prefer rice bowls then you will love my favorite menu item—it is also named the customer favorite—the Bee Beem Bhop in a hot stone pot. Steamed rice topped with your choice of meat, spinach, bean sprouts, shiitake mushrooms, zucchini, radish, cabbage, carrot, seaweed, butter, sesame seeds, sesame oil, and a fried egg quickly cooks on the hot stone pot. I prefer the short ribs or vegetables for my protein. The hot stone pot comes out steaming on a wood platter so that it doesn't burn the table. The steamed rice is quickly frying inside the hot pot, so it's important to keep stirring the food while eating. If the rice crisps to the side, it is easy to scrape off and makes it extra crunchy when you chew.

TIP

Don't order too much food. If you have an excessive amount of meat left over, you will be charged.

A single serving of the Korean barbecue is available but will be cooked in the kitchen and not left for you to make. The single-serving options include shrimp, scallops, or squid.

4 LA FILLETTE

LA FILLETTE, French for "little girl," is a French-inspired bakery on the outskirts of Congress Park. It's not just a French bakery but also a cozy spot to catch up with friends over a cup of coffee. The bakery is inviting from the smells to the decor. Right outside they have an A-frame sign with an arrow pointing toward the door that reads "Croissants" and another arrow pointing to the street with the words "No croissant." Choose wisely.

I could hang out here all day and eat. Owner Keturah Fleming's goal is to create classic French pastries well. However, she isn't afraid to add a hint of lavender or sage into something that normally wouldn't have it. It's her bit of dash paired with sass.

The front register has a large display of the pastries available for the day. One day might have quiches and macarons followed by sourdough breads and stuffed croissants the next. A few of the menu staples are le croissant: buttery and flaky layers of love; quiche lorraine: a mixture of eggs, flour, butter, milk, heavy cream, cheese, leeks and ham; les macarons: almond flour, sugar, egg whites, and flavoring; le pain au chocolat: similar to the croissant but stuffed with warm chocolate; and a rotation of artisan breads.

The egg and croissant sandwich—a fresh fried egg, choice of cheese, and meat layered inside a buttery croissant—made it in the local press as one of the *Westword* editors' 100 Favorite Dishes. You will not find any of the pastries short of butter; it's a staple in just about everything Fleming makes. The cinnamon roll is also made with flaky layers and a cream cheese frosting core. The cinnamon balances so well

TIP

CAN'T MAKE IT TO LA FILLETTE?

Get a taste of it at other Denver coffee shops like Logan House, Weathervane Cafe, and Onefold that carry La Fillette's pastries daily.

with the sugar. My favorite is the ham and gruyère cheese croissant for a post-meeting breakfast. Ask them to warm it up and savor a moment of relaxation as you slowly devour the croissant.

THE SOUTH BROADWAY CRAWL

1. **SUGAR BAKESHOP**, 277 Broadway, Denver, (720) 458-5432, sugar-bakeshop.com

2. **PUNCH BOWL SOCIAL**, 65 Broadway, Denver, (303) 765-2695, punchbowlsocial.com

3. **SWEET ACTION ICE CREAM**, 52 Broadway, Denver, (303) 282-4645, sweetactionicecream.com

4. **HISTORIANS ALE HOUSE**, 24 Broadway #102, Denver, (720) 479-8505, historiansalehouse.com

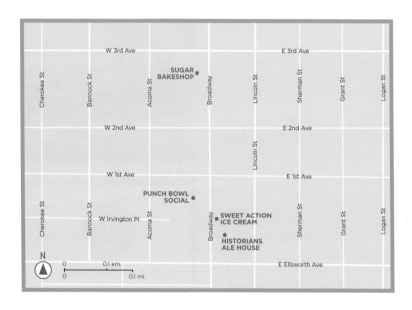

South Broadway

Brunchin' on Broadway

SOUTH BROADWAY IS HOME TO DOZENS of individually owned shops. This is the neighborhood everyone shops at for Small Business Saturday. There are over 20 female-owned establishments on the street too. This side of town used to be rugged decades ago and now it's living in its prime. For 10 blocks there are restaurants, breweries, yoga studios, coffee shops, and more restaurants. It's the perfect street to walk down when you're undecided on what to eat and want to see all your options. Broadway is one of the busiest streets in town, but you never have to wait to be seated for brunch. Now that's something to celebrate!

1

SUGAR BAKESHOP

Good vibes, sugar, and soul pour out of **SUGAR BAKESHOP**'s doors. The warm smiles from the team of early risers baking fresh pastries behind the counter are contagious. They live by their motto: "Sugar Bake: made for you, by us. From scratch. Every day." Still not convinced of all the love here? An old-school typewriter sits near the entrance to share good omens, love notes, motivational quotes, and funny confessions. They are posted on the windows and a perfect morning read after ordering.

Sugar Bakeshop is best known for the vegan popsters, their replica of a Pop-Tart, but better tasting and looking. The little handheld pastry is delicate and crispy on the edges. It's topped with frosting that matches the color of the filling inside. The strawberry, blueberry, and brown sugar cinnamon popsters are available year-round and can be found around town at other coffee shops. Seasonal flavors include raspberry pistachio, caramel apple, and red raspberry orange.

Other pastries available at the snack counter include lemon bars that sell out by the afternoon, muffins, cinnamon rolls, quick breads, scones, and their famous s'mores cookies. Anything remaining by the end of the day is put into the "Day Olds" basket for the next morning. These pastries are a deal and taste best dipped in hot coffee.

All pastries pair perfect with a coffee though, right? Sugar Bakeshop puts the same love into their coffee as they do their pastries. The menu covers standard hot drinks like drip coffee, cappuccinos, and hot tea. They stand apart from other coffee shops with their colorful lattes like matcha, beetroot, and golden milk, and their house-made infused syrups like rose cardamom, lavender, and vanilla.

TIP

SKIP THE PAPER CUPS, PLASTIC LID, AND HOT SLEEVE

The recycled mug shelf next to the register is for take-out coffee. Sugar Bakeshop's zero waste initiative lets customers take a mug and return it at their convenience.

2 PUNCH BOWL SOCIAL

This 27,000-square-foot gastro-diner is the ideal place to hang out on a snow day. **PUNCH BOWL SOCIAL** is the place to let out your inner child while sipping on the best cocktails. There's enough room for you and all your friends to pack the place and have entertainment all day. The main floor has darts, bowling, shuffleboard, and virtual reality games, while the upstairs has Ping-Pong, karaoke, pinball, and arcade games.

You'll never need to leave Punch Bowl, because not only can they keep you entertained, but they have a menu that covers all types of food. Share the Sheetload of Nachos made with adobo marinated squash, poblanos, tomatoes, black beans, monterey jack, queso, Cotija, crema, and salsa roja. The Superfood Grain Bowl is a flavor-packed salad with crispy farro, quinoa, kale, radishes, sprouts, pickled chiles, shiitake mushrooms, a poached egg, and miso ginger vinaigrette.

If I'm not at Punch Bowl for brunch, then my go-to menu item is the roasted chicken tacos: roasted chicken, salsa roja, oregano, monterey jack, shredded lettuce, and crema served on soft flour tortillas. Three come in an order and they are served with frijoles charros. Other favorites are the assortment of burgers or loading up on the shareables.

The Chicken 'N' Waffles are served during brunch and dinner. I prefer to eat them with brunch. Otherwise, I love the crispy crunch of the Duck Confit Huevos: chimayo red chile, black beans, crispy potatoes, corn tortillas, lettuce, tomato, onion, queso Cotija, and sunny-side up eggs.

Punch Bowl Social knows how to deliver great food, awesome service, and entertainment. I'm excited to see them expanding to other cities outside of Denver.

STRIKE OUT WITH A PUNCH BOWL!

Grab a ball, lace up those retro bowling shoes, and decide on a spirit with the crew. A punch bowl serves four or more people.

The Watermelon Polo Bowl:

Sauza Blue reposado tequila

Teakoe's watermelon spearmint tea

McClary Bro's watermelon shrub

House-made strawberry syrup and fresh lime juice

3
SWEET ACTION ICE CREAM

SWEET ACTION ICE CREAM has a half garage door they lift up daily to let the smell of fresh waffle cones hit the street. It's hard to walk by and not ponder what flavors are on the menu for the day. Since the ice cream is made in small batches, there are new flavors every day.

While you'll find vanilla bean on the menu, most other flavors are non-traditional like maple walnut caramel, green tea white chocolate chip, orange almond swirl, and salted butterscotch. They even carry two vegan flavors regularly. They make their non-vegan ice cream with all-natural Colorado dairy, causing it to be so creamy. They work with local purveyors, farmers, and bakers to source the produce for the unique flavors. Order your ice cream in a waffle cone, sugar cone, or a cup. Like all ice cream shops you can add sprinkles and the works.

If you love your flavor, you can take a pint to go. There is a freezer right by the line that has a variety of pints as well as ice cream sandwiches. Sweet Action makes it a priority to run a sustainable business. They are run entirely by wind power and all their packaging is compostable or recyclable.

4 HISTORIANS ALE HOUSE

In a street of bars and taverns stacked next to each other for blocks is a local hangout, **HISTORIANS ALE HOUSE**. They have a massive bar that runs the length of the restaurant with over 40 taps and a large selection of spirits. There's also a bar and seating upstairs on the rooftop. This is a spot you can come for a date night or show up looking for the bartender to cure your hangover.

I come to Historians for three main reasons: brunch, burgers, and cocktails. The best spot for brunch is on the rooftop with the build your own Bloody Mary bar. Choose from regular or spicy Bloody Mary mix and add your toppings like celery salt, celery, and cheese. The best entree to pair with a spicy Bloody Mary is the break-

fast burrito: a chipotle flour tortilla stuffed with scrambled eggs, cheddar, chorizo, and potatoes, then smothered in house-made pork green chili. This is a huge burrito and the most popular brunch item.

I also love visiting for the lunch special served Monday through Friday until 3 p.m. For $7.95 you get a cheeseburger and fries with the choice of a 10-ounce beer, well cocktail, or soda. The burgers are served in butchers' paper and tied with cheesecloth string. Once you open it up, get your taste buds ready for one of the best burgers in town. If you miss the lunch special, you can still get a burger on the dinner menu. Build your own or choose one of the signature options.

I love coming to Historians because the bar patrons are really nice. It's always a good crowd of people, and by the end of the night the barstool next to you might be filled with a new friend.

THE CHERRY CREEK CRAWL

1. **B&GC**, 245 Columbine St., Denver, (720) 925-8598, bandgcdenver.com

2. **QUALITY ITALIAN**, 241 Columbine St., Denver, (303) 532-8888, qualityitalian.com

3. **BLUE ISLAND OYSTER BAR AND SEAFOOD**, 2625 E. 2nd Ave., Denver, (303) 333-2462, blueislandoysterbar.com

4. **AVIANO COFFEE**, 244 Detroit St., Denver, (303) 399-8347, avianocoffee.blogspot.com

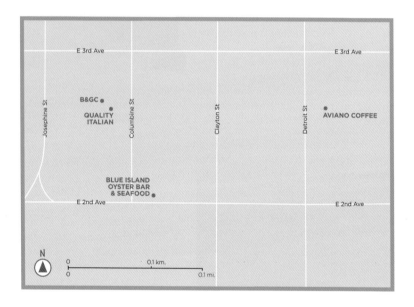

Cherry Creek

Paint the Town Red with Cherries

FLASH THE YACHT CLUB STYLE, Lamborghinis, and Louis Vuitton bags, Cherry Creek is for the rich and famous. It has premier shopping with over 160 shops and 20 eateries. The neighborhood is filled with renovated, modern homes and independent stand-alone stores in between art galleries, fitness studios, spas, and more. They celebrate their small business owners and connect them to residents to ensure their businesses flourish. Cherry Creek has a small-town feel, but it's a huge neighborhood within Denver and there's always new people to meet.

In the summer Cherry Creek hosts summer concert series, a food and wine festival, and an art festival. In the winter they host indoor sidewalk sales and a winter fest. There is always something happening. It's best to explore this side of town as a pedestrian or by bicycle.

1

B&GC

Shhhh, this is a speakeasy. The highly sought-after secret membership can skip you to the front of the line, but otherwise there are specific instructions for getting into **B&GC**. Text, don't call, after 3 p.m. on the day you'd like to visit. Reservations for other days will be ignored. Give them specific details: name, party size, and preferred time. If you have followed the steps carefully, you will receive a confirmation text with instructions on how to enter.

Somewhere, since I can't tell you exactly where, in the alley is a private gold doorbell. Press that and you will be greeted by a staff member who will take you through the hallways and down to the basement of the former Cherry Creek Post Office. When the door opens, let your eyes adjust to the dim Edison bulb lighting and the flashy art deco bar. B&GC is a clandestine bar that transports you to the Prohibition era. Let loose and get lost in the experience.

Each cocktail is inventive and carefully curated. There is a booklet available with all the spirits and cocktails available like a French75 or Old Fashioned, but your server will create a drink to fit your preferences. A few quick questions about spirits and aromas will help concoct the perfect cocktail.

TIP

If you're looking for an Instagrammable cocktail, order the deconstructed dirty martini. You will be given all the tools to mix it yourself. The vodka comes in a mini glass container on ice, with olives on the side and a chilled glass.

2 QUALITY ITALIAN

New York City's favorite Italian steakhouse, **QUALITY ITALIAN**, opened a second location in downtown Cherry Creek attached to Halcyon Hotel. Reclaimed wood doors and industrial accents are noted upon entering, but the wine storage and bar in the middle of the restaurant will quickly capture your eye.

The house wines are exclusively made for the restaurant out of California wineries. QI's wine list is extensive with over 250 bins from around the world to select from. Occasionally they will have a blind choice bottle of wine, typically a variety they are discontinuing (or running out of) that is offered at a deep discount. I highly recommend choosing the red or white option.

My favorite entree on the menu is the Quality Chicken Parm, in the form of a pizza. The crust is made out of ground chicken and breaded before it is put into a deep fryer. It's then layered with marinara and cheese before it is broiled to perfection. The chicken parm is sliced into pizza triangles and served with

honey and arugula. If this is too indulgent for you, try the Spicy Lobster Rigatoni alla Vodka. It's fired tableside with the house-made pasta.

Come for the weekend brunch and bottomless Bellinis. The signature Bellini cart will serve you tableside with seasonal flavors like grapefruit and pomegranate, cucumber lime, or classic white peach. The Bellinis pair deliciously with the Polenta Pancakes with the lemon ricotta and blueberry compote.

3 BLUE ISLAND OYSTER BAR AND SEAFOOD

New England ambience has docked in Denver at **BLUE ISLAND OYSTER BAR AND SEAFOOD**. The atmosphere is casual, and the culture is inspired by childhood memories on the East Coast. Daily shipments of seasonal oysters and seafood are sent from Blue Island Shellfish Farms in Long Island, New York. This ensures the quality and allows the seafood to be priced reasonably.

Blue Island is open for weekend brunch and daily lunch, happy hour, and dinner. It would be salty to not order oysters from the raw bar. Wire baskets with chalkboard signs are overflowing with different oysters, chilled on shaved ice. You can walk right up and pick your oysters out.

The clam chowder is made New England style with sea clam fritters and apple-smoked bacon. It will be award worthy whenever Denver decides to put it to the test against other clam chowders. During lunch you can order the signature lobster roll with a cup of clam chowder. Order the lobster roll hot and buttered. You won't regret this decision.

Have you ever wanted to learn to shuck oysters and clams? The last Sunday of every month is the Chef and Shucker Class. You're given guided instructions on the art of shucking followed by your own dozen to give it your best shot. The class includes a glass of wine, small bites, appetizer, and an oyster shucking knife.

If you're there for dinner, share the ¼-pound P&E shrimp served with Old Bay and cocktail and hot mustard sauces. Atlantic cod fish-and-chips is a filling dinner entree with cracker crust and shoestring fries. Wash down all the fish with a hand-crafted cocktail or pair it with a wine. The staff will guide you through the best pairing options.

Celebrating? Blue Island will make your night exceptionally special. Let the host know when making a reservation. They will have something up their sleeve to commemorate your evening.

4

AVIANO COFFEE

AVIANO COFFEE is so popular in Cherry Creek that they have two locations. Detroit Street is the original location catering to the locals, while the St. Paul Street location is thoughtfully located between several hotels. Aviano always has a line out the door, a full patio, and very few spots to sit inside. That's because it's the place to be. Meet friends, say hi to acquaintances, or grab a coffee to go, but never come if you don't want to socialize.

They serve Intelligentsia coffee at both locations. If you're looking for an individual experience, connect with your cup through a pour-over coffee. Watch as the barista waters the filter, steams water for the hot beans, and then pours over. Slowly and carefully, your cup will begin to release the aromatics. The staff here has mastered the art of making perfect coffee.

My go-to at Aviano is the oat milk latte with the house-made syrup. They typically have vanilla syrup, simple syrup, and a seasonal flavor. I pair it with an almond croissant. It's buttery and flaky with a gooey inside of almond paste. There is always a small offering of fresh-baked, daily pastries.

THE WASH PARK CRAWL

1. **HOMEGROWN TAP & DOUGH,** 1001 S. Gaylord St., Denver, (720) 459-8736, tapanddough.com

2. **DEVIL'S FOOD BAKERY,** 1004 S. Gaylord St., Denver, (303) 777-9555, devilsfooddenver.com

3. **BONNIE BRAE ICE CREAM,** 799 S. University Blvd., Denver, (303) 777-0808, bonniebraeicecream.com

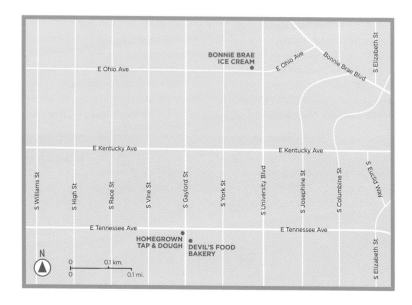

Wash Park

Chic Boutiques and Eateries

WASHINGTON PARK, BETTER KNOWN AS WASH PARK, is a booming residential area that surrounds a massive park that has separate areas for cyclists, pedestrians, and cars. Volleyball nets and yard games fill the east side of the park, tennis courts and B-cycle stations on the south, the historic Washington Park Boathouse and flowerbeds to the west, and the lake to the north. When the sun sets, the neighborhood moves to Old South Gaylord Street Shops with its chic boutiques like Wish, Barbara & Co, and W Boutique and the restaurants in between.

1 HOMEGROWN TAP & DOUGH

HOMEGROWN TAP & DOUGH was the vision of co-owner Jean-Philippe Failyau. He was on a mission to share his love for pasta with Old South Gaylord Street. The space came first and had a wood-fired oven inside, which led to an easy move toward pizza and pasta. His next mission was to find an affordable price point and keep neighbors coming back. You'll quickly notice they have accomplished that with the This Round Is on Me board where neighbors can buy a drink for each other and write it up on the board to be redeemed on the next visit.

The menu started with pasta favorites like rigatoni Bolognese (house-meat sauce, shaved parmesan, basil, and sausage) and mushroom fusilli (truffle Alfredo, spicy sausage, parmesan, roasted mushrooms, and parsley). Recently, it has added healthier options like the Zucchini Noodle Primavera: artichokes, spinach, roasted tomatoes, pine nuts, black olives, and ricotta cheese.

There's plenty of fun for kids at the free arcade in the mini hut on the patio. It reminds co-owner Peter Newlin of playing Ninja Turtles at Pizza Hut during his childhood. He wants to give the neighborhood kids the same memories. If you can't peel yourself away from the games, order the crispy chicken wings Italian-style with pepperoni, pepperoncini, parmesan, and marinara. Nosh on those until you're ready to go inside for the rest of your meal.

Pizza favorites include the "Pete"Za named after Newlin's favorite toppings: red sauce, candied bacon, ham, pineapple, and jalapeño; the classic Nonna: garlic oil, roasted tomatoes, smoked mozzarella, burrata cheese, and parmesan; or the Pigs and Pear: roasted garlic base, mozzarella, goat cheese, butternut squash, candied pears, candied bacon, grated parmesan, arugula, and balsamic drizzle.

The coolest part of the restaurant is the local furniture sourced from craftsmen. Scott Bennett, from Housefish, played a huge part in interior design features like the ski lift chair booth. And the photos on the wall are part of the history of Colorado photo archives from the Colorado History Center. The restaurant purchased the rights to the photos so they could be enlarged and displayed.

2 DEVIL'S FOOD BAKERY

Pastries, coffee, and tea fill this adorable bakery. This is a branch of the original **DEVIL'S FOOD**, now called Devil's Food Cookery. While the cookery serves breakfast and lunch in an eclectic spot, the bakery welcomes the morning crowd to watch through the tiny window panes as the bakers make breads, quick breads, croissants, and more.

All the items are moved to the front glass cases to tempt anyone who comes inside. The cookies are ginormous and soft. They are still gooey throughout the day. The cupcakes look too perfect to touch with their rose-patterned frosting, but sink your teeth into them. They're soft inside and if you arrive early enough, some are still warm. The muffins fly off the shelf before 11 a.m. because everyone knows to grab a muffin with a latte. The coffee served here is from Sweet Bloom Coffee Roasters, located in Lakewood, Colorado. Order an espresso or coffee to pair with a sweet treat.

Everything about Devil's Food Bakery's ambience makes you feel like you're sitting at a cafe in Paris. The ceiling shines with antique tin tiles, pink plaid wallpaper fills the walls, and 100-year-old barn wood covers the floors. There's even a National cash register; it doesn't get more vintage than this antique piece on the counter.

3

BONNIE BRAE ICE CREAM

For over 30 years **BONNIE BRAE ICE CREAM** has been serving cones to the community. The ice cream is made in house and flavors are picked in store or influenced by customers. There's always a line out the door, because it is hard to choose which flavor to pick from when they offer 32 options. Classics like vanilla, mint chocolate chip, cookie dough, and strawberry are always available. It's the fun flavors like Cashew Divine, Grand Marnier Chocolate Chip, French Silk, and Udder Budder that everyone must sample.

You can get your scoop in a cup, waffle cone, sugar cone, or sundae. A waffle cone dipped in chocolate with Oreos is my top choice. I add a scoop of B-Twixt, a version of Twix in vanilla ice cream, and a second scoop of cupcake. Bonnie Brae also serves vegan ice cream, sorbet, and frozen yogurt.

If you love their desserts as much as the rest of Denver, you can order a pie: your choice of ice cream flavor scooped into a cookie crumb crust; or an ice cream cake. They always have a freezer full of cakes to purchase for any special occasion, or you can make a special order with different ice cream flavors.

THE PLATT PARK CRAWL

1. **CHOOK CHARCOAL CHICKEN**, 1300 S. Pearl St., Denver, (303) 282-8399, chookchicken.com

2. OTOTO, 1501 S. Pearl St., Denver, (303) 733-2503, ototoden.com

3. **UNO MAS TAQUERIA Y CANTINA**, 1585 S. Pearl St., Denver, (303) 777-2866, unomastaqueria.com

4. **STEAM ESPRESSO BAR**, 1801 S. Pearl St., Denver, (303) 952-9716, steamespressobar.com

5. **MARIA EMPANADA**, 1298 S. Broadway, Denver, (303) 934-2221, mariaempanada.com

6. **PARK BURGER**, 1890 S. Pearl St., Denver, (720) 242-9951, parkburger.com

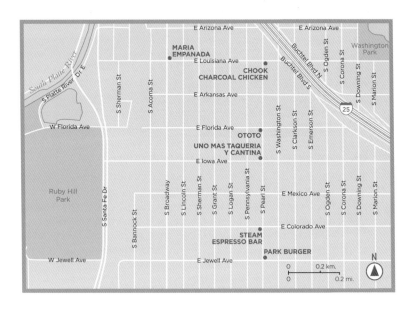

Platt Park

The World Is Your Oyster on Pearl Street

PLATT PARK IS DEFINED BY OLD SOUTH PEARL STREET and the established families who reside there. Kids ride up and down the streets on their bicycles and many families own dogs. Every Sunday in the summers the farmers' market takes over the whole street for multiple blocks. Residents come early to fill their bags with fresh produce and head to Steam Espresso Bar for their morning coffee. This southern Denver neighborhood is quiet on weeknights with restaurants closing by 10 p.m. However, they have an incredible food scene with Maria Empanada, OTOTO, and the recently opened Chook Charcoal Chicken. The restaurants all have different price points and most have their own kid-friendly spaces. Platt Park is best known for Karma Yoga studio and the original Park Burger.

1

CHOOK CHARCOAL CHICKEN

The newest concept by Alex Seidel and Adam Schlegel can't be missed in the Platt Park neighborhood. **CHOOK**, slang for chicken in Australia, roasts chickens over a charcoal rotisserie at affordable prices. Chook is a place that is about more than the food. It is about the community and making decisions that will impact everyone. Chook is a B-corp restaurant that focuses on recyclable material, farming responsibly, and planting trees as they are removing trees. One percent of sales is given back to the community. Once you order, you are

given a blue token to drop into one of the three glass jars that represent the charities of the month.

The food at Chook is what also sets this restaurant apart from the rest of the Denver food scene. Executive chef Aaron Whitcomb, named one of the

CERTIFIED B CORPORATION

Chook is a B-corp restaurant. According to the Certified B Corp website, "Certified B Corporations are a new kind of business that balances purpose and profit. They are legally required to consider the impact of their decisions on their workers, customers, suppliers, community, and the environment. This is a community of leaders, driving a global movement of people using business as a force for good."

best chefs from *Best Chefs America*, heads the back of house and keeps the food tasting its best. Order a quarter, half, or whole chicken from the menu with the choice of two sides. My top choices are the Celery-Apple Slaw: celery root, cabbage, carrots, and fennel seed vinaigrette; the Pacific Dinner Rolls: a perfectly crafted Hawaiian sweet roll by Füdmill bakery; and the Chook Wedges: Colorado potatoes, Chook chicken salt, and choice of sauce. If I had to pick one thing to eat every day for the rest of my life, I'd eat the Avocado Chicken Sandwich made with the chilled pulled rotisserie chicken, avocado, cucumber, cilantro, and skyr-lime aioli served on grilled ciabatta.

Guests can also order online, park in the designated pickup window space, and carry out. This makes it convenient for a parent to grab and go without unloading their kids. If you prefer to make food at home or want another taste of Chook, then pick up the Booyah Kit: broth, vegetables, grains, and instructions to make a stew.

2 OTOTO

OTOTO is one of the three Japanese-inspired restaurants on Pearl Street, all owned by the same restaurant group, Den Corner. Owners Toshi and Yasu Kizaki opened OTOTO as the younger brother to their first concept, Sushi Den. They wanted OTOTO to capture a more casual ambience. The menu includes a raw bar, ramen, rice bowls, and robata grilled skewers.

JAPANESE STREET FAIR!

Every summer Den Corner hosts the Summer Rooftop Party to indulge in ramen, hand rolls, and *yayai* (Japanese street food). Ototo, Sushi Den, and Izakaya Den fly 12 elite chefs to Denver from Japan to make their best dish for people to try. It's one of the coolest food events in town, with bottomless sake and Japanese spirit–inspired cocktails.

The service is top-notch. Listen to the daily chef's specials from the fresh fish shipment flown in from the Sea of Japan less than 24 hours ago. The best way to experience everything on the menu is to bring a few friends and order as much as possible. Start with a few small plates like agedashi tofu: lightly cornstarch dusted and fried pieces of tofu, mountain yams, Japanese eggplant, and shishito pepper, finished with daikon oroshi and fresh scallions in a tempura sauce; the Japanese Chicken Kara-Age: marinated dark meat dusted in potato flour and fried, shishito pepper and Kara-Age aioli; and the grilled whole squid: Japanese yari-ika "Spear" squid sprinkled with seaweed flakes, sesame seeds, and lemon. A lighter option is the sashimi, eight pieces of the freshly caught "catch of the day" from the raw bar.

Next, move on to the entrees. The ramen is house made and available daily. Order the tonkotsu ramen: pork belly, wood ear mushrooms, green onion, garlic chips, bok choy, and a soft-boiled egg in a savory 48-hour pork broth. Another ramen favorite is miso ramen: pork belly, sweet grilled corn, bok choy, bean sprouts, and a soft-boiled egg in a savory 48-hour steeped miso pork broth. If it's too warm for ramen, order from the rice bowls. A best seller is the unagi bowl made with barbecued freshwater eel over teriyaki-glazed rice and finished with a side of kinpira.

Save room for dessert. You can drink your dessert with the Yuzu Cream Pie Martini: vanilla vodka, yuzu, and simple cream; or eat the traditional mochi cake served with green tea mochi ice cream.

3

UNO MAS TAQUERIA Y CANTINA

The smell of smoked meats and the energetic ambience will stop you in your tracks on the sidewalk. Enter **UNO MAS TAQUERIA Y CANTINA** and you will immediately feel at home. The meats are so tender because they are smoked from 4 to 13 hours. The vegetables topped on the meats are locally sourced and taste crisp. Uno Mas Taqueria y Cantina encourages neighbors to donate their extra produce to them from their at-home gardens instead of letting it wilt away. Each dish is made with love, and you will be able to taste it.

The Pearl Street location was their first and opened in 2013. It has become so popular that they have expanded to two additional locations. Everyone craves the Mexican fare and the 70 small-batch tequilas. On the menu you will find traditional tacos like carne asada: grilled lime and garlic–marinated skirt steak, salsa verde, crispy potato, and poblanos; or al pastor: chili de arbol y pineapple–marinated Duroc pork and poblano radish slaw. However, there are inventive tacos like Sea of Cortez: chile-rubbed sea scallops and shrimp, fresh avocado, cilantro, ranchero salsa, and Cotija cheese. The menu also includes tortas, posole, and salads. Accompany your meal with a margarita or venture into the old-world tequila selections made with blue agave. If you aren't familiar with tequila, ask the server or bartender to tour you through the best options. The staff is knowledgeable and passionate about the tequilas. They even spend time in Jalisco, Mexico, harvesting blue agave plants and touring distilleries to immerse themselves in the culture that shaped the region.

4 STEAM ESPRESSO BAR

STEAM is a neighborhood gem that is always calmly busy. Don't believe me? Babies fall asleep in their strollers to the sound of the espresso beans grinding, conversations are kept to a low chatter, and customers with laptops rarely need headphones to drown out the sound. The front door is constantly welcoming and waving off customers who grab coffee on their morning walks. I'd say they put something in their coffee, but they do; they serve ethically sourced beans from micro-roasters. Premium coffee is paired with sustainable brewing techniques for each perfect cup.

Outside remnants of a vintage airplane stick out of the ground and wildflowers create a tiny oasis. The patio is always full from the concrete bleachers to the bistro tables. Occasionally a band will perform on the patio while people sip lattes. A walk-up window from the patio quickly keeps the line moving. If you know what you like, skip the indoor line and go express.

Steam serves coffee from Boxcar, a local roaster in Boulder, and pastries from Trompeau Bakery. They do not offer a full service menu but light bites to get you through your craving. If coffee isn't your thing, they make fresh-pressed juices with vegetables and fruits. The flavors of the juices are always changing based on what is available, but they typically offer two varieties.

5

MARIA EMPANADA

With only $300 in her pocket and on a mission to live the American Dream, owner Lorena Cantarovici arrived in the United States without knowing a word of English. She reminisced about her dreamy childhood in Argentina eating empanadas at family gatherings. Empanadas, little handheld pockets of dough stuffed with hot ingredients, could be found anywhere on the streets of Cordoba. How had Denverites never had empanadas, and why was everyone asking what it was? These questions were the genesis of Lorena's small bakery. As the business picked up, she expanded into her garage and eventually into a commercial space that is the home of the first sit-down **MARIA EMPANADA**.

The empanadas are only half of what I love about this place. The other half is the employees. Everyone loves their job and they love to share it with you. I've salsa danced with staff members and drank wine with their wine distributors. When you are at Maria Empanada, you are welcomed home like family.

Empanadas are baked fresh daily by hand. Breakfast empanadas are available in the morning until 10:30 a.m. or when sold out. Flavors range from the Egg & Potato to the Spanish Chorizo: eggs, potato, cheese, salsa, and chorizo Español. After breakfast 11 savory empanadas are available, like the Argentina: tender seared steak, eggs, red peppers, and green onions; or the Corn: sweet corn, spices, and cheese sauce.

There is more on the menu than empanadas. You can order tartas, the Argentinian version of a quiche, Spanish tortillas, and dessert. Order a bottle of wine and stay a while. You may stumble upon a night of bachata dancing or live music.

6 PARK BURGER

PARK BURGER is housed in a former chocolate shop that owner/executive chef Jean-Philippe Failyau purchased in 2009. He was looking for a casual, family-friendly restaurant in the neighborhood when he stumbled across the location. It was perfect with 40 seats and a prime location. Now it's an award-winning burger bar that was recognized as one of the top 10 new burger restaurants in 2010 by *Bon Appétit* magazine, Winner of Best Burger—Judges' Choice in the Denver Burger Battle in 2010, 2011, and 2013, and Best Burger—Editors' Choice in 2010 in *5280* magazine.

The awards go to the natural, never frozen patties. The Park Burger menu offers turkey, veggie, beef, and buffalo patties that are served on locally

baked buns. The Royale, a ⅓-pound patty with caramelized onions, blue cheese, and bacon, is one of the bestsellers, as is the El Chilango, a ⅓-pound patty with cheddar, jalapeño, and guacamole. The burgers are inventive; for example the Scarpone: beef patty, provolone, crispy pancetta, giardiniera, and truffled garlic aioli. People can't get enough of the mixture of toppings. You can add a fried egg, sautéed mushrooms, haystack onions, Italian pancetta, bacon, and more to your burger.

Park Burger is so popular in Denver that they have continued to expand from the original Platt Park location. They now have four locations spread across the Denver neighborhoods in LoHi, RiNo, and Hilltop, a neighborhood next to Cherry Creek.

THE UNIVERSITY CRAWL

1. **SNOWLAB**, 4360 E. Evans Ave., Denver, (720) 772-8475, snowlabco.com

2. **MUSTARD'S LAST STAND**, 2081 S. University Blvd., Denver, (303) 722-7936, mustardslaststandcolorado.com

3. **JELLY CAFE**, 1700 Evans Ave., Denver, (720) 596-4108, eatmorejelly.com

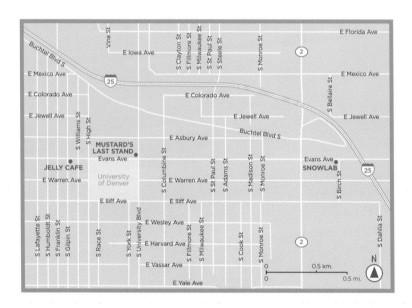

It's a Law to Eat Good Food

THE UNIVERSITY NEIGHBORHOOD surrounds the University of Denver, known for its prestigious law program and lacrosse team. Coffee shops, pubs, and late-night eateries serve the college crowd, but locals flock to places that have been in the neighborhood for decades like Mustard's Last Stand. University Avenue is full of apartments and strip malls. but behind all those tall buildings are some cute, single-family bungalows and parks. The University neighborhood is quiet and shadowed by large trees once you step off the main street.

1

SNOWLAB

SNOWLAB has brought the West Coast's hottest, or shall I say coolest, dessert to Denver. Shaved snow originated in Taiwan and is a creamy ribbon-like dessert. It's also known as *xue hua bing*. It's not ice cream nor frozen yogurt. It's its own category of frozen dessert, made from fresh and natural ingredients. SNOWLAB's shaved snow is never made from powders like other competitors. It comes in a bowl and is almost weightless until the toppings are added.

First you choose your base flavor choice. The shaved snow flavors include black sesame, chocolate, avocado, chrysanthemum, coconut, coffee, Earl Grey, Thai tea, and tamarind. Next you choose your toppings. The first section of toppings include traditional items like dragon eyes—a Southern Asian fruit similar to lychee but less aromatic, grass jelly, lychee jelly, mango boba, and mini mochi while the second section has toppings similar to fro-yo: strawberries, M&M's, gummy bears, crushed Oreos, and assorted cereals. The final step is your choice of drizzle. The condensed milk is my favorite option but there's also caramel, chocolate, raspberry, mango, and coconut condensed milk. You can create your own flavor combinations, but the staff is happy to help if you need guidance.

If you're unsure of what to order, start with the shaved snow combination menu. A popular go-to is Avocado Alps: avocado shaved snow, dragon eyes, and mango boba topped with condensed milk. Another option is Mount Coffee: coffee shaved snow, coffee jelly, chocolate chips, and caramel drizzle. Or try the Strawberry Sierra: strawberry shaved snow, strawberries, and strawberry boba with condensed milk.

MUSTARD'S LAST STAND

For more than 40 years, **MUSTARD'S LAST STAND** has been serving Chicago-style hot dogs and food to Denver and Boulder. This location is in a pastel yellow house with brick red shutters and Vienna Beef umbrellas on every patio table. It's hard to miss it from the road.

> These sausages embody Chicago. The tradition, the teams, the fans, the big appetites. Chicago deserves a monster sausage they can be proud of.
>
> —*Mike Ditka, Chicago Bears Hall of Fame player*

Chicagoans love Mustard's because they serve a true Chicago-style hot dog with yellow mustard, relish, onions, tomato, pickle, sport peppers, celery salt, and Chicago bright green relish. They also offer Polish sausage with mustard, relish, onions, tomatoes, pickles, hot peppers, and sauerkraut; and Italian beef with thin-sliced roast beef, Italian-style gravy, cooked green peppers, giardiniera, hot peppers, and grilled onions. The menu even nods to Chicago Bears Hall of Famer Mike Ditka with the Ditka ⅓-pound Monster Polish: an 8-inch sausage served on French bread.

The menu continues with other favorites like the charbroiled burgers (order a single or a double), sandwiches, meatless options, and a kids' menu. Dining at Mustard's isn't satisfactory until you order the hand-cut french fries. These spuds are sprinkled with the perfect amount of salt and served piping hot. Add dipping sauces like cheese, Jamaican jerk, parmesan ranch, and more. You can even get messy and smother them in vegetarian chili with shredded cheese.

There are so many great options that you'll soon be a regular at Mustard's Last Stand.

3 JELLY CAFE

JELLY CAFE flips pancakes and fries doughnuts daily for the brunch crowd. Their goal: eat more jelly. Salad, sandwiches, and burgers are available but no one comes to Jelly to eat lunch. This is one of the hottest breakfast spots in town!

Buttermilk pancakes rule the plates with single, double, and even triple stacks. Lavender Blueberry pancakes are blueberry pancakes topped with homemade lavender blueberry preserves while the Bacon is buttermilk pancakes griddled with bacon crumbles and served with strip of bacon on top. Don't fret, they also have french toast. The Molly Hot Brown is seared turkey served on savory french toast, smothered in poblano cheese sauce, and topped with bacon and griddled tomatoes; this might seem like a wild combination, but it is found under the "Favorites" on the menu.

Not everyone loves pancakes in the morning, so if you're that person, they have Benedicts, scrambles, hashes, and more. The smoked salmon Benedict is the winner in my opinion: two griddled salmon fillets and two perfectly poached eggs are served over artisan sourdough bread and covered with dill hollandaise. If you choose a hash, select the sweet potato hash: Mexican chorizo, onion, celery, roasted poblano pepper, red potatoes, and sweet potatoes served with two eggs any style and choice of

TIP

Always order the dough-nut bites. They pop into your mouth in one perfect bite, so if the 4-doughnut-bite portion is too small, upgrade to the large with 8. Daily flavors: cinnamon sugar, crème anglaise, jelly-filled, lemon-filled, maple bacon, Mexican choco-late, salted caramel, and Thai peanut.

toast. Prepare to unbutton your pants with the Ultimate Biscuits & Gravy: sausage gravy, bacon, caramelized onions, tomato, and cheddar cheese served with rustic potatoes and two eggs any style.

Jelly Cafe is a staple in Denver with a second location in Capitol Hill. They maximize on space with tight seating, so prepare to share your bacon with your neighbor. The decor is amusing with vintage cereal boxes, flamboyant colored menus, and teacup chandeliers. Sit back and take in all the fun. The only thing you need to worry about is if you are craving sweet or savory. All the options are satisfy-ing, so only you can decide.

THE GREEN CHILI CRAWL

1. **EL TACO DE MEXICO**, 714 Santa Fe Dr., Denver, (303) 623-3926, eltacodemexicodenver.com

2. **SANTIAGO'S**, 5 locations (see website for details), eatatsantiagos.com

3. **WORK & CLASS**, 2500 Larimer St., Denver, (303) 292-0700, workandclassdenver.com

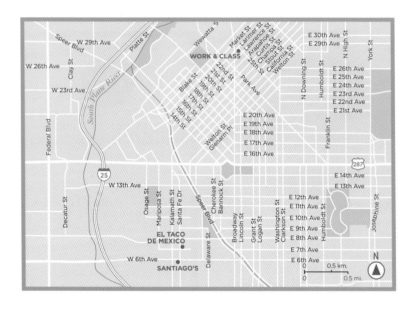

Bonus Crawls!

Green Chili

IF THERE'S ONE THING THAT'S UNIQUE to the Denver food scene, it's green chili. I can't tell you which is the best, because there will never be a consensus. Every restaurant has its own version. Green chili should not be confused with red or bean-style chili; it is something that you smother, dip, or lather on your food. I say "something" because it comes in every form of salsa, sauce, soup, and condiment. The versions vary from soup to chunky, vegetarian or traditional pork, gluten free or with a flour base. Chain restaurants that originate out of state but have Colorado locations adapt to the Colorado craving and serve their own green chili, such as Shake Shack, which created the Green Chili CheddarShack burger. One final note about the famed green chili: New Mexico and Colorado do not get along on this topic, nor will they ever. Mayors and state representatives have continually battled over who should be named the official Green Chili State. The difference is Hatch versus Pueblo chiles, but the history of this argument goes well beyond the type of chiles used.

1 EL TACO DE MEXICO

The soupy and vibrant green chili from **EL TACO DE MEXICO** is a blended stew. The pork fat glistens with red spice flecks. The flavors of smoke and garlic stand out the most.

2 SANTIAGO'S

The orange-colored green chili has thick diced peppers. It can be ordered mild, hot, or half and half—the mild tones down the hot green chili.

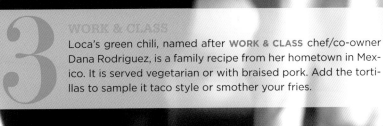

Loca's green chili, named after **WORK & CLASS** chef/co-owner Dana Rodriguez, is a family recipe from her hometown in Mexico. It is served vegetarian or with braised pork. Add the tortillas to sample it taco style or smother your fries.

THE FOOD HALLS AND MARKETPLACES CRAWL

1. **AVANTI FOOD & BEVERAGE**, 3200 Pecos St., Denver, (720) 269-4778, avantifandb.com

2. **DENVER MILK MARKET**, 1800 Wazee St., #100, Denver, (303) 792-8242, denvermilkmarket.com

3. **DENVER UNION STATION**, 1701 Wynkoop St., Denver, (303) 592-6712, unionstationindenver.com

4. **DENVER CENTRAL MARKET**, 2669 Larimer St., Denver, denvercentralmarket.com

5. **STANLEY MARKETPLACE**, 2501 N. Dallas St., Aurora, stanleymarketplace.com/marketplace

6. **ZEPPELIN STATION**, 3501 Wazee St., Denver, (720) 460-1978, zeppelinstation.com

7. **THE SOURCE HOTEL + MARKET HALL**, 3350 Brighton Blvd., Denver, (720) 443-1135, thesourcehotel.com

8. **THE BROADWAY MARKET**, 950 Broadway, Denver, (720) 390-7132, broadwaymarketdenver.com

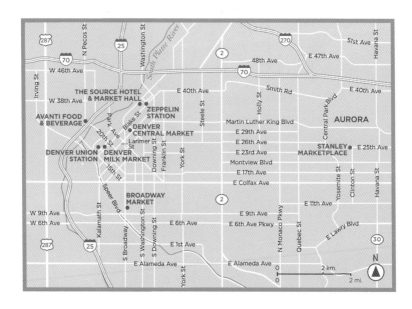

Bonus Crawl!

Food Halls and Marketplaces

FOOD HALLS AREN'T A NEW CONCEPT, but the way Denver is building them and executing their interiors has made it the ultimate leader for other cities. The food halls are packed with people meeting before going out, celebratory moments, date nights, and more. They encapsulate the whole community with different cuisines at each restaurant. The halls vary from family friendly to co-working space to those suited for the gastronome to a few that are heavily bar focused. Regardless of what you might be looking for, every Denver food hall is worth checking out because no two halls are alike.

AVANTI FOOD & BEVERAGE

AVANTI F&B is situated in LoHi with a rooftop facing Coors Field baseball stadium and the Denver skyline. It's a collective eatery consisting of seven different restaurant concepts at affordable prices. Each food stand is in a shipping container with a shared kitchen prep space. The first floor houses five concepts while the upstairs has two. Quiero Arepas is one of the longest-standing tenants and my personal favorite. They serve Venezuelan-style arepas, a corn-based flat pita stuffed with ingredients that fits in your hand for easy transport. Pro-tip: order the passion fruit juice from Quiero Arepas and add a single or double shot of alcohol to it.

The coolest and most convenient thing Avanti offers is the option to share your bar tab between the upper and lower floors. This is ideal on a busy night when the lower bar is a quick way to grab a drink to enjoy while finding a spot on the rooftop.

2 DENVER MILK MARKET

Longtime local chef/owner Frank Bonanno and his wife Jacqueline created **MILK MARKET** to be their lasting legacy in the Denver culinary scene with 16 restaurant concepts. Located in the historic Windsor Dairy building of LoDo, each concept represents Frank's best dishes from his other stand-alone restaurants around Denver.

Ruth's Butchery and Albina by the Sea pay homage to both Jacqueline and Frank's mothers while Bonanno Brothers Pizzeria nods to the whole family. Jacqueline's mother, Ruth Drake, left behind a handwritten cookbook from 1929 with many of the current recipes. My favorite item is the Classic Reuben with pastrami, corned beef, sauerkraut, swiss, Russian dressing, and Jewish rye bread. Albina's Crab Cake and Blackened Tuna dishes are inspired by Frank's mother's love for baking fresh bread to accompany the fresh-caught fish from the shore.

The market is open daily with concepts for the morning rush and others for the late-night crowd. The early risers can start their morning with Frank's popular crumb cake and a cup of coffee from Morning Jones while the night owls can snag a pizza by the slice at Engine Room with a cocktail at Moo Bar.

Explore the alley with motivational signs decorated from the brick walkway to the illuminated ceilings. Most Instagrammed plaques include: "You are cleverly disguised as a responsible adult," and, "Sometimes you win, sometimes you learn."

3 DENVER UNION STATION

DENVER'S UNION STATION is the main transportation hub for the Metra, light rail, RTD buses, and more. The station opened in 1881 but closed after a fire and reopened in the current building in 1914. It was vacant for decades and was renovated in 2012. Union Station is more than a transportation center; it's a small representation of Denver. It's a place to hang out with friends and family or a hub to collect your out-of-town visitors when the airport is too far of a drive.

The Terminal Bar, housed in the former ticketing window, serves the best spicy Bloody Mary and light bites from ACME, a delicatessen and pizzeria. If a craft cocktail is calling your name, the Cooper Lounge located on the mezzanine floor has the best overlook of the station. It's hip and has sumptuous bites of food to kick off the evening or savor a nightcap.

Union Station has an array of small boutiques in addition to restaurants, like Tattered Cover Book Store, a locally owned indie bookstore, and 5 Green Boxes, an eclectic mix of one-of-a-kind gifts.

4 DENVER CENTRAL MARKET

Located in Denver's RiNo district, this 14,000-square-foot market has 11 vendors inside offering a range of sweet and savory options. Coffee shop vibes from Crema Bodega start the mornings and Curio bar attracts the afternoon and evening crowd to the energetic marketplace, a place to gather, shop, or host a meeting.

The smell of the Sin-amon Roll from Izzio Bakery can't be missed in the mornings, while the wood-fired pizzas from chef Andrea Frizzi's Vero Italian take over in the evening. The There are multiple food vendors like chef Justin Brunson's Culture Meat & Cheese; Tammen's, a fish market; Green Seed Market, a produce grocer; and The Local Butcher.

A visit to **DENVER CENTRAL MARKET** isn't complete without an Ice Kouign sandwich. This famous pastry from Izzio Bakery with a thick scoop of ice cream in between from High Point Creamery became a Denver icon after *Zagat* and *Vogue* covered it in their national publications.

5 STANLEY MARKETPLACE

This community-inspired marketplace was conceived by a few neighbors as a beer hall and has become home to more than 50 merchants. **STANLEY MARKETPLACE** is located between two different neighborhoods and has brought the community together with their Stanifesto: "Stanley Marketplace is where people go to live: to eat, drink, work, play, learn, grow, gather and explore, to see friends and make new ones. We're Stanley. And we're here for good."

A few favorites mentioned in earlier chapters have an additional location in Stanley such as Maria Empanada, Rosenberg's Bagels, and Sweet Cow Ice Cream. Pedicures from Base Coat Salon pair perfectly with a glass of wine from Infinite Monkey Theorem, or you can burn off the samoa doughnut from Glazed and Confused at Endorphin group fitness class.

Reserve a half-day for a visit to Stanley, because the collection of Denver's best restaurants all in one spot is hard to beat. Try the yeasted waffle with seasonal fruit from Annette, or The Situation taco with slow-cooked sirloin from Comida Cantina.

6 ZEPPELIN STATION

This food hall features eight vendors. It's a collection of innovative chefs, merchants, and creative companies all housed under one roof. Kiss + Ride is the main bar that greets customers. Modeled after a European train station bar, it was created to be a place to grab a drink while walking around.

7 THE SOURCE HOTEL + MARKET HALL

THE SOURCE, in the RiNo neighborhood, is a one-stop foodie destination with marketplaces. Twenty-five artisans fill the market including a butchery, flower shop, brewery, art gallery, and barbershop. The restaurants are top-notch at The Source, and it can be hard to pick which one to eat at. Longtime tenant Acorn dishes up seasonal, family-style plates. They boast an oak-fired oven and grill for their entrees like the wagyu beef. Safta, a modern Israeli restaurant from James Beard Award–winning chef Alon Shaya, is always filled with people because of the unlimited pita bread served with house-made hummus. The Bulgarian Lamb Kebab is a must-order item. Head to the rooftop at The Woods for New Belgium Brewing craft beers paired with featured dishes. Sleep off the food coma at the Source Hotel and enjoy the panoramic views of the Rocky Mountains from the Japanese soaking tub.

8 THE BROADWAY MARKET

On the busy Broadway Street, connecting Capitol Hill with South Broadway, is the newest food hall, **THE BROADWAY MARKET**, a celebration of renowned Denver chefs like Daniel Asher, Biju Thomas, and Lorena Cantarovici. There are nine concepts and a variety of cuisines for everyone. The Broadway Market is a zero-waste food hall inspired by the village food halls around the world.

Set up at the Broadway Bar or walk around from vendor to vendor. Maria Empanada has an additional location here, and the majority of other vendors—Miette et Chocolate and the Mondo Mini market among them—have locations in the Stanley Marketplace. Stand-alone concepts include Royal Rooster, which serves chicken sandwiches and burgers, Mother Tongue, which brings the exploratory flavors of Ottoman-inspired street food, and Pizza Coperta, offering Roman pizzas and street food.

DATING SCENE CRAWL

1. **COOHILLS**, 1400 Wewatta St., Denver, (303) 623-5700, coohills.com

2. **MERCURY CAFÉ**, 2199 California St., Denver, (303) 294-9258, mercurycafe.com

3. **HABIT DOUGHNUT DISPENSARY**, 2200 California St., Denver, (720) 428-8565, habitdoughnuts.com

4. **THE 1UP ARCADE BAR**, 1925 Blake St., Denver, the1uparcadebar.com

5. **SO DAMN GOUDA**, 2432 W. 44th Ave., Denver, (303) 455-2221, sodamngouda.com

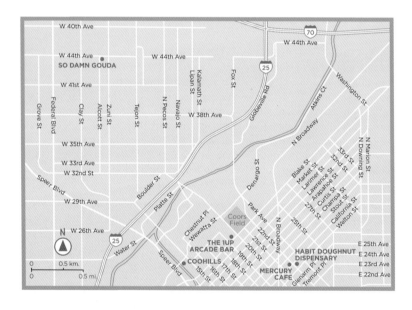

Bonus Crawl!

Dating Scene

DENVER, OFTEN REFERRED TO AS MENVER, has a reputation for having more single men than single women. For those seeking men, the dating scene of this city is sizzling hot even during the coldest months. What's the catch? Dating doesn't only revolve around the casual first-date coffee and second-date dinner with a movie. It's rock climbing, riding bikes down the Cherry Creek bike path, listening to the Colorado Symphony play '80s music, spiking a volleyball at Wash Park, two-stepping at the Grizzly Rose, a midnight screening at the Esquire Theater, or day trip to backcountry skiing on Berthoud Pass. There are a million perfect dates in Denver—some seasonal—that you can pair with a bite to eat.

1, 2

DARE TO BE DARLING DOWNTOWN
Peruse the art at the Museum of Contemporary Art (aka the MCA) with rotating artists. Head to the rooftop bar to toast the sunset. Keep the night going at **COOHILLS** restaurant around the corner, then catch a laugh at Voodoo Comedy Playhouse's improv night.

Take swing dance lessons at **MERCURY CAFÉ** and bond over the Jitterbug and Lindy Hop.

3-5

Enjoy a late-night doughnut and a nightcap at **HABIT DOUGHNUT DISPENSARY**, because dessert comes first on dates.

Nosh on some chicken wings and compete in skee-ball at **THE 1UP ARCADE BAR**. This adult arcade has the best pinball machine selection in town and classic video games. Complete the evening with a concert at Summit Music Hall.

Pick up a cheese board and chocolates from **SO DAMN GOUDA**, and park at the Denver Mart Drive In theater for one or all three film features.

THE BOULDER CRAWL

1. **BLACKBELLY MARKET**, 1606 Conestoga St. #3, Boulder, (303) 247-1000, blackbelly.com

2. **CORRIDA**, 1023 Walnut St. #400, Boulder, (303) 444-1333, corridaboulder.com

3. **SANTO**, 1265 Alpine Ave., Boulder, (303) 442-6100, santoboulder.com

4. **BASTA**, 3601 Arapahoe Ave., Boulder, (303) 997-8775, bastaboulder.com

5. **FRASCA FOOD & WINE**, 1738 Pearl St., Boulder, (303) 442-6966, frascafoodandwine.com

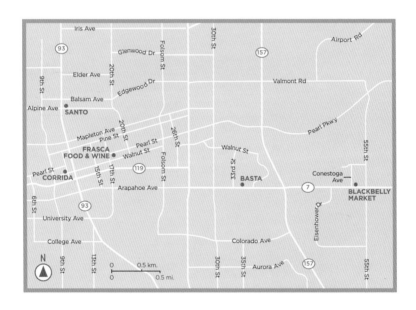

Bonus Crawl!

Boulder

WHILE SOME MIGHT ARGUE THAT BOULDER is 30 minutes too far outside of Denver, others would claim that a trip to Colorado isn't complete without a visit. It sits between the western plains and the foothills of the Rocky Mountains. The best view is anywhere from town, looking west at the iconic Flatirons. Boulder takes pride in its hiking and biking trails, outdoor lifestyle, and hippie culture. It's a town filled with activities, from floating down the river to shopping at the farmers' market. If there's one thing Boulder should be on the map for, it's their food scene. While my food crawl list could be as long as this book, these are a few of my favorite spots.

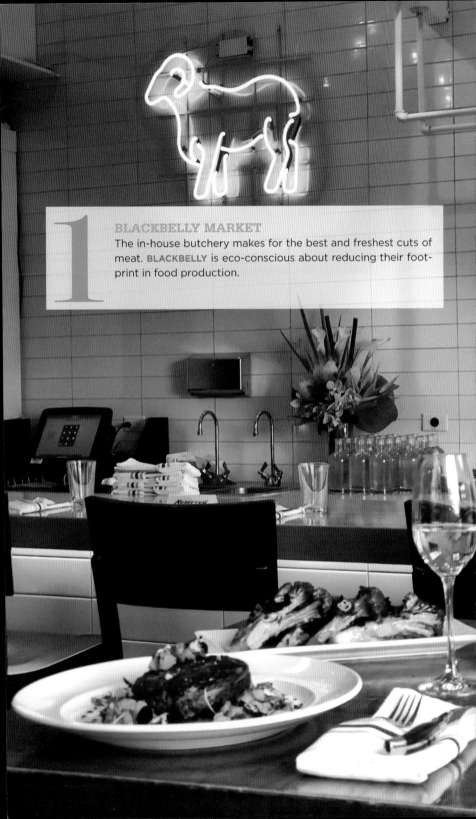

1

BLACKBELLY MARKET

The in-house butchery makes for the best and freshest cuts of meat. **BLACKBELLY** is eco-conscious about reducing their footprint in food production.

2

CORRIDA

Influenced by northern Spain's Basque country, **CORRIDA** focuses on wood-fired steaks. I highly recommend brunch and the bar cart service.

SANTO

Don't hold back on the morning libations; the Margarita Fresca features house-made fruit purees. The menu at **SANTO** is New Mexican–inspired.

4

BASTA

The best way to experience **BASTA** is through the family-style tasting menu. You'll taste oysters, salads, breads, cold plates, hot plates, pizza, and more.

5

FRASCA FOOD & WINE

It's still unbelievable how such an amazing restaurant is so close to get to. **FRASCA** serves the Friulano cuisine and fine wine from Italy.

THE GOLDEN CRAWL

1. **MINERS SALOON**, 1109 Miners Alley, Golden, (303) 993-3850, miners-saloon.com

2. **OLD CAPITOL GRILL & SMOKEHOUSE**, 1122 Washington Ave., Golden, (303) 279-6390, oldcapitolgrill-smokehouse.com

3. **ABEJAS**, 807 13th St., Golden, (303) 952-9745, abejasgolden.com

4. **CHEESE RANCH**, 601 16th St., Golden, (303) 278-1293, cheeseranch.com

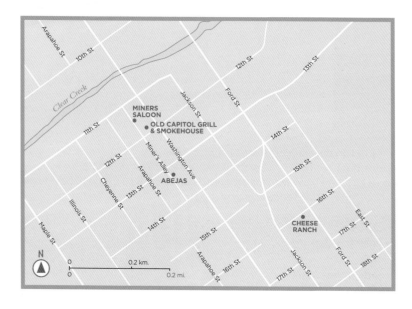

Bonus Crawl!

Golden

HOME OF THE SILVER BULLET, Colorado School of Mines, and Buffalo Bill's grave, the town of Golden is a place for everyone. Entering into the town, at the corner of 12th Street and Washington Avenue the large, over-arching sign greets you with "Howdy Folks. Welcome to Golden. Where the West Lives." The old-town charm from this former mining town is reflected on the exterior of the historic buildings, but the trendy store interiors attract boutique shoppers. At sunset the town of Golden transforms into a lustering glow with the mountains as its backdrop. The patios bustle with cyclists, students, and longtime residents.

1

MINERS SALOON

After a long bike ride, this is the place I stop to refuel. **MINERS SALOON** is tucked away in an alley. The decor evokes the late-1800s mining days in the town. It's a modern vibe with rustic accents like the old oil lamps and mining tools hanging on the wall. A cozy fireplace in the middle of the restaurant separates the dining room and the bar. The bar is positioned in the front of the restaurant with views of the sunset while the dining room is dimly lit in the back.

The bar has 24 taps of beer and the signature Miner's Margarita on the last tap. It's strong but delicious and refreshing. For a heartier option try the chili dog: wild game chili and Welsh white cheddar served with a Coors Light beer. Miners Saloon offers a variety of shareable plates to start and paninis or sandwiches for the main entrees.

2

OLD CAPITOL GRILL & SMOKEHOUSE

This restaurant is in the former Capitol build-ing and can be found on the main street: Washington Avenue. The building has the old western saloon look on the outside and wraps around the street in an L-shape. The interior carries that ambience with the original brick walls, antique pendant lights, and a massive wood bar as the backdrop. The beer selection is what you can expect out of any Colorado bar, a long list covering pilsners to IPAs.

The menu includes steaks, smoked meats like brisket or baby back ribs, burgers, and Colorado trout: pan seared, with roasted cau-liflower and potatoes. For those seeking lighter fare, the appetizers include an array of bar bites.

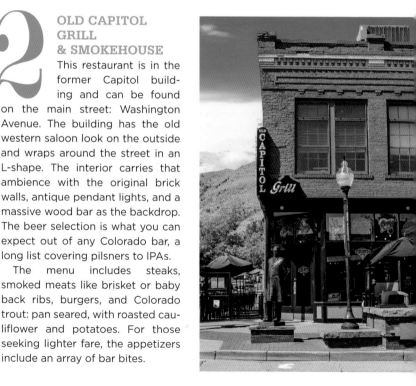

3

ABEJAS

This downtown Golden restaurant serves seasonal items. They focus on sustainable fish, local produce, and organic meats. The menu contains an assortment of foods, but if you call it Colorado cuisine, that would best describe it. Sample offerings include duck confit hash with Tokyo turnips, snap peas, potatoes, poached egg, and toast; pan-roasted ruby trout with apricot farro, roasted radicchio, mâche, green romesco, and herb vinaigrette; lamb chop with farro, sun-dried tomatoes, eggplant, cucumber, turmeric white bean puree, and leek yogurt; or the house-made sausage with mashed potatoes, red sauerkraut, braised greens, and spicy mustard.

ABEJAS RESTAURANT is the prime spot to enjoy tea and coffee in the morning or a cocktail to celebrate a milestone.

4

CHEESE RANCH

The locals told me about **CHEESE RANCH**, and now I have to share it too. It's an artisan deli located in a strip mall; look for the fun, changing cheese chalkboard. The store is filled with cheese wheels and deli cases. They serve charcuterie boards complete with Marcona almonds, dried apricots, jams, meats, and of course, a variety of cheese. The menu has six types of cheese boards and a build-your-own option. That's not all they serve though; there is an extensive list of hot and cold sandwiches including paninis. The Dago sandwich includes Italian meats, cheese, and stuff—your toppings; the Bay of Pigs is Cubano-style with three types of pig, cheese, and stuff. Grab and go or stay and pair your meal with a beer or wine.

Acknowledgments

I HAVE TO START BY THANKING my amazing fiancé, Neil Phippen. He crafted many Old Fashioneds for me when I was trying to meet deadlines. Thank you, Neil, for being my book sherpa.

To my mom, Christy Patterson, I don't know which one of us was more excited about this opportunity. Thank you for immediately delegating yourself as my book tour manager.

Thanks to Rebecca Durigan for capturing candid moments and being willing to drop everything for a photo shoot. Thank you, Trey Bryant, for your incredible skyline photos. Thanks to all the Colorado foodies, who are famous on Instagram, and donated their photos to this book: Alexa Moor with World Is My Menu; Ashley Garcia and Christian Selby with Hungry Hungry Hipsters; Jimena Zamora with Comino Food Stories; Julie Rodriguez with Julie Likes Food; and Laura Young with New Denizen Blog.

Hand modeling can be tough. Hot dishes, awkward angles, outfit changes, and nicely manicured nails are just a few of the behind-the-scenes obstacles that made all these photos happen. Blair Douglas, Laura Fritz, Ashley Garcia, and Bailey Rhatigan, I appreciate you!

A huge shout-out to all the public relations agencies: B Public Relations, Sprocket, ROOT Marketing & PR, and Feed Media. Thanks for helping me get all my facts straight and put me in front of the chefs and restaurant owners.

Thank you to everyone at Globe Pequot, an imprint of The Rowman & Littlefield Publishing Group, Inc. Special thanks to Katie O'Dell and Sarah Parke, my amazing editors, for being patient with my deadlines and always hopping on the phone to chat through a tough moment; Amanda Wilson for the beautiful cover design and working through my edit requests; and Melissa Baker, my compass and the best cartographer, for assisting me in the map designs.

Finally, to all the chefs, back-of-house crews, restaurant owners, managers, and front-of-house crews who let me invade their spaces to capture photos and gather information for this book. You're my #HospitalityHeroes. Thank you for helping my taste buds explore new flavors and dishes.

Having all of you believe in me to write this book has been astonishing. I have an amazing support system.

Photo Credits

All photos by Bre Patterson except the following:

Trey Bryant: p. i

Getty Images: pp. iii (brianbalster), 193 (welcomia)

Ashley Garcia, @hungryhungryhipsters: pp. iv (2nd from top, bottom), 17, 18, 56, 57 (bottom left), 65 (top), 102, 120, and 145 (bottom)

Alexa Morr, @worldismymenu: pp. v (bottom), 23 (top left), 51, 54, 70, 71, 75, 146 (bottom), 147, 148, and 195

Laura Young, NewDenizen.com: p. 76

Julia Rodriguez: pp. 77 (bottom), 109

McCall Burau, McCall Burau Photography: pp. 112, 113

Rebecca Durigan, Rebecca Christine Photography: pp. 198, 216

Jimena Zamora, @cominofoodstories: p. 206

Index

About the Author

BRE PATTERSON is the foodie behind Bites with Bre. She was born and raised in the Chicago suburbs and will always be a Cubs fan first, Rockies fan second.

At a young age she was encouraged to explore food and the different ingredients that make a dish. She hosted cooking shows for her mom at their kitchen island and attended Friday fish boils and fries with her dad every weekend to critique the different dishes from restaurant to restaurant. She always had a camera to document her food adventures whether at home or a restaurant.

Bre's passion has always been in the food and beverage world. She earned a bachelor's of food science

at Colorado State University and quickly moved her way through hospitality management roles after college. At the age of 25, she became a general manager and would upload photos of the new restaurant menu on her Instagram (around 2015). It was just a fun and creative outlet to share food. A few years later, Bre shifted her personal Instagram into Bites with Bre.

Quickly after, she launched her blog and was recognized as a new outlet for sharing food by PR companies. She remembers the first time she was invited as a guest to The Broadmoor; she felt like she had made it. Eventually, her friends, family, and colleagues encouraged her to take her Bites with Bre full-time in 2017. Bre loves to share stories she hears from the chefs, farmers, restaurant owners, and staff while dining out and taking photos around her new hometown, Denver, Colorado.